To my mother

Understanding Keynes

AN ANALYSIS OF 'THE GENERAL THEORY'

John Fender

LECTURER IN ECONOMICS, UNIVERSITY OF LANCASTER

Wheatsheaf
Books

A MEMBER OF THE HARVESTER PRESS GROUP

First published in Great Britain in 1981 by
WHEATSHEAF BOOKS LTD
A MEMBER OF THE HARVESTER PRESS GROUP
Publisher: John Spiers
Director of Publications: Edward Elgar
16 Ship Street, Brighton, Sussex

© John Fender, 1981

British Library Cataloguing in Publication Data
Fender, John
  Understanding Keynes.
  I. Title
  330.15'6   HB99.7
  ISBN 0-7108-0110-6

Printed in Great Britain by
St Edmundsbury Press,
Bury St Edmunds, Suffolk
from typesetting by
Alacrity Phototypesetters,
Banwell Castle, Weston-super-Mare

HARDBACH A7PAPCL PRILo £5.95

nich this was

Understanding Keynes

AN ANALYSIS OF 'THE GENERAL THEORY'

Contents

Preface

This book is intended to provide, as its title states, an analysis of John Maynard Keynes's *The General Theory of Employment, Interest and Money*. As such, it will hopefully be of interest to advanced undergraduates studying macro-economics and monetary economics, and to postgraduates and professional economists interested in macro-economics and disequilibrium theory as well as in the slightly narrower area of Keynesian exegesis.

My thoughts on the interpretation of Keynes have evolved over a number of years. Over this period, I have received encouragement, advice and criticism from a number of people, and in this context I would like to thank V. N. Balasubramanyam, John Flemming, David Gowland, Nicholas Oulton, Robert Rothschild, Peter Sinclair and Paul Stoneman as well as participants in seminars at Oxford, Lancaster, Reading and York. Needless to say, none of the above is at all responsible for any errors, mistakes or inaccuracies in the work for which I take full responsibility.

I am most grateful to the Royal Economic Society and Macmillan, London and Basingstoke and St. Martin's Press, Inc., New York, for permission to quote from Keynes's *General Theory of Employment, Interest and Money*, *Tract on Monetary Reform* and *Treatise on Money*.

I am also most grateful to the many people who at various stages struggled to type the book, including Stephanie Arkwright and Adele Anscombe, and to Christa Gausden, who was most helpful with the proofs.

John Fender
Lancaster University
March 1981

1 Introduction: The Classical System

John Maynard Keynes's *The General Theory of Employment, Interest and Money* (Macmillan, 1936, henceforth cited in references as G.T.) made a major, indeed revolutionary impact on economic theory, and its impact was not confined merely to the academic world; indeed, as Keynes predicted, it has revolutionized 'the way the world thinks about economic problems' (see G.T., back cover). Although the extent of the overall impact of the book on government economic policy is debateable, it would be absurd to deny that its influence has been considerable and it has been commonplace to regard the economic policies of most Western post-war governments as dominated by Keynesian thinking. One is reminded of Keynes's comment that 'Madmen in authority ... are distilling their frenzy from some academic scribbler of a few years back' (G.T. p. 383).

However, the exact nature of the theoretical contribution made by Keynes has been the subject of considerable dispute. Post-publication criticism eventually led to the emergence of the so-called neoclassical synthesis, according to which Keynesian economics was a special case of neoclassical economics, derived by imposing the special assumption of money wage rigidity. The claim that an under-employment equilibrium could exist in the absence of money wage rigidity was argued to be false and to depend upon a failure to take into account the wealth effect on consumption of a lower price level (the Pigou effect). But it was also argued that the special assumption made by Keynes happens to be relevant for the world in which we live, so that Keynesian economics *is* relevant for policy. But this consensus was destroyed by the work of Clower and Leijonhufvud — the principal references here are Clower (1965) and Leijonhufvud (1968). The upshot seems to be that even today, more than forty years after the publication of the General Theory, there is no consensus in the economics profession on the precise theoretical contribution made by Keynes. For example, Patinkin writes: 'forty years later disagreements continue to go on in the literature about the role played by such crucial assumptions as wage rigidities, the liquidity trap, the interest inelasticity of investment, unemployment equilibrium and the like' (Patinkin, 1976, p. 23) and Weintraub writes: 'Unfortunately, there is today no accepted view of what it was that Keynes actually accomplished' (Weintraub, 1979, p. 38). Hence, the exact nature of the theoretical contribution made by Keynes has been the subject of considerable dispute.

The aim of this book is to put forward what is claimed to be a new interpretation of Keynes's work, and also to criticize preceding interpretations from the standpoint of the interpretation propounded. It is not claimed that the approach is entirely original; many elements which have featured in previous interpretations of Keynes, topics such as money, uncertainty, the consumption function, money illusion, expectations, disequilibrium, etc., will all feature in the interpretation presented here; it is claimed, however, that the way these diverse elements are integrated to produce an overall interpretation is novel.

It is hoped that the work will not just be of exegetical interest, although the major aim of the work is exegetical. It may be relevant for contemporary economics for three reasons. First, it may enable an assessment of the relevance of Keynesian economics for the present day to be given (this will be discussed in the final chapter). Secondly, it might be said that the work of Clower and Leijonhufvud, although primarily exegetical, stimulated the development of the disequilibrium model building of such authors as Barro and Grossman. Hopefully the present work, by drawing attention to different features of the economic system might induce work on these features of the system. Thirdly, in expounding Keynes, various theoretical concepts will be used and discussed. It is hoped that the exposition and clarification of these concepts might be of some value. Nevertheless, the main aim of the present work is exegetical; whether it achieves any of these further ends is to some extent incidental to the main purpose of the book.

A contention which will surely be raised in discussing any attempt to produce an interpretation of Keynes is that there is already a surfeit of literature in the area and that further attempts are likely to run into rapidly diminishing, if not negative, returns. However, the fact that there may be a great deal of literature in an area does not preclude further contributions; for later contributions may serve to synthesize, evaluate and improve upon earlier contributions. The crucial question is, of course, whether previous literature in the area has produced a satisfactory interpretation or not; if the answer to this question is negative, then there must be room for further contributions. It has already been suggested that there is no existing adequate interpretation of Keynes's General Theory; whether the present interpretation improves upon previous interpretations is not for the author to judge. But there is no *a priori* case for ruling out subsequent contributions on the grounds that there have been a large number of previous contributions.

Moreover, the author would like to dispute the notion, which seems quite common, that there has been a vast number of contributions in the area, which is now reaching saturation point. It is perhaps possible to divide recent contributions into three categories. First, there is the work of Leijonhufvud and Clower, and the critical work which this has inspired (for example, Grossman, 1972; Bliss, 1976; Jackman, 1974; Flemming, 1974), but it does not seem that there have been a large number of important contributions in this area. Secondly, there is the literature which has been inspired by the gradual publication of Keynes's collected works; the major reference here is Patinkin (1976). This is arguably the best piece of work which has been produced on Keynesian economics; however, it does not seem to solve, or even attempt to solve, the problem which is confronted *here*, namely that of constructing an interpretation of Keynes's G.T. which incorporates all the diverse elements which are believed to be of importance in Keynesian economics. Thirdly, there is the work of authors such as Davidson and Minsky (see Davidson, 1978; Minsky, 1975) but such works seem to embody a particular, somewhat idiosyncratic point of view which has not gained widespread support. Very recently, a number of further contributions have appeared: Brenner (1979), Chick (1978) and Chakrabati (1979). It is perhaps too early to come to a proper assessment of these works;

however, none seems to take an approach similar to that taken here. Apart from these aforementioned contributions, the author is unaware of any recent, important interpretation of Keynes's General Theory.

The primary intention of this book is to provide an interpretation of Keynes's General Theory; the author feels that the procedure of concentrating on the General Theory to the relative neglect of Keynes's other works can be justified. It is this book which has had the major impact on post-war economic thought and which embodies the essence of what is now known as Keynesian economics. As has already been suggested, there has been no entirely satisfactory interpretation of the General Theory so far and an analysis of this can be valuable not only from the point of view of the history of economic thought, but also for present-day economic controversies. Nevertheless, the change in Keynes's thought from his earlier writings is perhaps of some interest and may shed some light on the structure of the General Theory itself; for this reason a chapter on the development of Keynes's thought has been added.

In the remainder of this introductory chapter, the theory which Keynes attacked and sought to replace as a theory of output, employment and money, the so-called 'classical theory', will be discussed. A taxonomy of previous interpretations of Keynes will be presented and discussed, and a brief outline of the approach to be taken in this book will be given.

The 'classical theory' may be represented by the following equations:

$$N^D = N^D(w/p) \tag{1.1}$$
$$N^S = N^S(w/p) \tag{1.2}$$
$$N^D = N^S \tag{1.3}$$
$$Y = f(N^D) \tag{1.4}$$
$$C(Y, i) + I(i) = Y \tag{1.5}$$
$$m/p = g(Y, i) \tag{1.6}$$

Alternatively, define $\bar{N}$ as the value of N which satisfies equation (1.3). Then define $\bar{Y}$ by $\bar{Y} = f(\bar{N})$.

Then replace equation (1.4) by

$$Y = \bar{Y} \tag{1.4'}$$

and delete equations (1.1) to (1.3).

Equations (1.1) and (1.2) state that the supply of and demand for labour are both functions of the real wage. Equation (1.3) states that the labour market clears; the real wage is such that the quantity of labour which workers wish to supply at that real wage is equal to the quantity employers demand. Equations (1.1) to (1.3) are basically equivalent to the two classical postulates which Keynes discusses in chapter 2 of the General Theory. Equation (1.4) enables us to infer the full employment level of output from the level of full employment; it is a short-run production function, with employment as its sole argument; this is a relatively uncontentious element of classical theory, at least as far as comparison with Keynesian economics is concerned. Equation (1.5) determines the allocation of output between consumption and investment. The idea is that the rate of interest adjusts in order to ensure that the level of investment is equal to the level of savings at full employment. This is the classical theory of the rate of interest which Keynes discusses and attacks in his chapter 14. Equation (1.6) enables the price level to be determined; in such an economy the quantity theory of money will hold, in the sense that a change in the money stock will induce a proportionate change in the price level. An alternative underpinning to the classical system is provided by Say's Law — equation (1.4'). Say's Law is not normally stated this way; indeed, it is rarely, if ever, stated in an equational form or linked with the rest of the classical system. However, as stated it has the implications attributed to it both by the classical economists and by Keynes; it will be discussed more fully, and the interpretation given here will be defended at greater length in chapter 3. It is a statement that the full employment level of output will be continuously maintained, but it is an argument which focuses on the output market, not on the labour market.

Consumption and the demand for money have both been written as functions of both income and the rate of interest. However, it would be fair to say that the classical economists did not stress the dependence of consumption on income or of the demand for money on the interest rate, so much so that one might characterize their position as excluding these variables from the relevant functions. However, it is perhaps hard to believe that a classical economist would not accept that if the national income doubled, there would be no increase in consumption or that he would not be prepared to concede some interest elasticity in the demand for money function. For example, Keynes writes, referring to the classical economists: 'they would, presumably, not wish to deny that the level of income also has an important influence on the amount saved' (G.T., p.178) and Patinkin devotes an Appendix of his *Money, Interest and Prices* to arguing that the classical economists did believe that 'the demand for money was sensitive to the rate of interest' (Patinkin, 1965, pp.630-4). However, the classical economist would certainly not stress these factors and the question whether these factors should be incorporated into the relevant functions will be left open. Keynes certainly did stress these factors; whether he should be characterized as differing from the classics in the emphasis placed upon these factors or in incorporating them into functions which previously did not contain them as arguments, is not a question which will concern us here. In the course of the book reasons will be given for the classical school's relative neglect of these factors.

It has sometimes been argued that Keynes was unfair to the classical economists and that the picture he presented of classical economics was a mere caricature; for example: 'The Keynesian definition of classical economics was ... tendentious and egocentric' (Sowell, 1974, p.5). It is impossible to discuss this question comprehensively in a book of this kind; however, the following points may be relevant.

There are several points where Keynes seems to take pains to represent the classical economists correctly. He devotes an appendix (the appendix to chapter 14) to discussing Marshall and Ricardo's theory of the rate of interest, and another appendix (that to chapter 19) to arguing that Pigou's views on unemployment fall into the classical tradition. Nevertheless, Keynes does complain from time to time that he can find no explicit statement of the classical doctrine. For example, in discussing the classical theory of the Rate of Interest, he writes: 'I find it difficult to state it precisely or to discover an explicit account of it in the leading treatises of the modern classical school' (G.T., p.175). And having described what he takes to be the classical theory of the rate of interest, he writes: 'the above is not to be found in Marshall's *Principles* in so many words. Yet his theory seems to be this, and it is what I myself was brought up on and what I taught for many years to others' (*ibid.*). So Keynes does seem to take some trouble to portray the views of the classical economists; moreover, they are views which he once held.

Perhaps the major reason why it has been felt that Keynes caricatured the classical economists was that their thought was much more sophisticated than that contained in the six equations described earlier in the chapter. However, we should remember that Keynes was not attempting to portray the whole of classical economic thought; his concern was with characterizing the theoretical framework underlying their thought.

The theory, as described earlier in the chapter, does generate many of the ideas which one associates with the classical school. For example, if the government increases its spending, this will lead either to a fall in private sector investment or in consumption or in both, and if consumption spending is interest-inelastic there will be 100 per cent crowding-out of the private sector investment — the so-called 'Treasury View'.

The framework is, moreover, a fairly straightforward application of the market-clearing paradigm — which has had such a strong hold on economists' imaginations to the macroeconomy. The variables which feature in the framework, variables such as consumption, investment and the interest rate, are the variables which economists are often interested in when they look at the macroeconomy, and the theory provides a plausible account of how they are determined, given the assumption that markets clear.

Finally, on the classical theory, there does not seem to be any significantly different representation of the classical theory which has attracted widespread support. A possible counter-example is the representation of the classical system given in Hicks (1937). It will be argued in chapter 8, though, that this is an incorrect representation of the classical theory; moreover the author is unaware of any support that Hicks's version of classical economics has attracted.

So, for the reasons given above, the author would reject the view that Keynes was unfair to and caricatured the classical school and would contend that his representation of the theoretical framework underlying classical economic thought was basically correct. However, whether Keynes was fair or not to the classical economists is somewhat irrelevant as far as the main purpose of this book is concerned. Given that the set of equations (1.1) to (1.6) embodies what Keynes thought constituted classical economics, our main concern will be to characterize the way(s) in which Keynes differed, and how he proceeded to construct his own theory.

Many different interpretations have been given of precisely how and where Keynes differed from the classical theory. Below a taxonomy of interpretations which have appeared in the literature is presented; it does not pretend to be exhaustive, but at least it does try to cover the main points of view which have been put forward:

1.   Keynes assumed that workers were subject to 'money illusion'. Hence labour supply is a function of monetary, as well as of real, variables. One representation of money illusion might be to incorporate money wages, as well as real wages, in the labour supply function. Hence the so-called 'classical dichotomy' no longer holds; a change in the quantity of money may change the volume of employment as well as changing prices. This is because the equilibrium volume of employment will change; the labour market continues to clear. This interpretation can be attributed to Leontief (see Leontief, 1936).

2.   Keynes assumed that money wage rates were rigid in a downwards direction; this might be because of money illusion on the part of the workers (though an argument is necessary to link money illusion and wage rigidity) or because of institutional reasons. Hence we have the additional equation

$$w = \bar{w}.$$

In order to prevent the system from becoming over-determined, the labour market equilibrium condition (equation (1.3)) is relaxed and employment is given by

$$N = \min (N^d, N^s)$$

which is a conventional assumption about the determination of quantities traded when markets do not clear. This is a fairly commonplace interpretation of Keynes; it will be discussed in chapter 2.

3.   Keynes denied that equation (1.5) has a solution, when Y is the full employment level of output (given that the interest rate must be non-negative). Hence the classical system has no equilibrium (see Klein, 1966, pp. 84-5).

4.   Keynes emphasized the role of the rate of interest in equation (1.6); he also argued that the demand for money function might have a special form so that the demand for money might become perfectly elastic at some positive interest rate (the liquidity trap). This minimum interest rate might be above that given by equation (1.5) so that again the classical system has no equilibrium.

5.   Keynes emphasized the role of income in equation (1.5) as an argument of the consumption function.

6.   He emphasized the role of uncertainty in the economy; in the more extreme formulations of this view, no equational format can capture Keynes's essential insights. Coddington calls those Keynesians who take such a point of view 'fundamentalists' (see Coddington, 1976, pp. 1259-63). Loasby seems to express such a point of view when he writes: 'unemployment in a market economy is a result of ignorance too great to be borne'. (Loasby, 1976, p. 167). A more moderate formulation of this view would emphasize the implications of uncertainty for investment and the demand for money.

7.   Keynes emphasized the role of money in the economy. For example, in the introduction to the General Theory, he writes: 'a monetary economy ... is essentially one in which changing views about the future are capable of influencing the quantity of employment and not merely its direction' (G.T., p. vii). But it is not clear how such a viewpoint should induce us to change the classical theory as outlined in equations (1.1)-(1.6).

8.   Keynes denied the validity of Say's Law.

So there seem to be a multitude of interpretations of Keynes in circulation, and the above list in no way pretends to be comprehensive.

In the course of this book, it will become possible to pronounce upon the correctness of these interpretations. The position taken will be closest to the position (2), in that the appropriate equational representation of the Keynesian system will be that specified in that paragraph. But the interpretation presented here will not be that Keynes assumed money wage rigidity. Rather, it is that he gave reasons for relaxing the labour market assumption, or at least for considering an economy in which this assumption need not hold. To complete the model an exogenous (not a rigid) money wage is postulated. This position is closely related to the IS/LM interpretation of the General Theory, and it will be argued that IS/LM does indeed present a possible schematization of Keynes's theory. However, IS/LM goes back to Hick's 1937 article (see Hicks, 1937) and the reader would be justified in wondering where the element of novelty in the present interpretation lies, if the author is just reaffirming an interpretation presented over forty years ago. One might equally well ask why Hicks's interpretation did not gain immediate and widespread acceptance. The answer is, I think, that there has been the continual suspicion that there is more, perhaps much more, to the General Theory than that contained in the IS/LM framework. Topics such as uncertainty, expectations, money illusion, wage rigidity etc., have all featured prominently in discussions of Keynesian economics and it is rather difficult to see how they can be incorporated within an IS/LM type framework. What this book will attempt to do is to show how all the diverse elements which are believed to be important in the General Theory can be fitted together to produce a coherent interpretation of the book. This has not to my knowledge been done, or even attempted before. So, in a sense, there is something in all the views presented above; what the interpretation presented here tries to do is to show how they can be incorporated into a coherent overall picture of what Keynes was doing in his General Theory.

Perhaps a brief outline of the interpretation of Keynes to be given in this book would be useful at this juncture.

In chapter 2, an interpretation of Keynes's views on the labour market is presented. He is attacking the classical theory's views on the labour market, according to which the quantity of employment is determined by the intersection of the supply and demand curves for labour. Keynes has two objections to this equilibrium theory of the labour market. The first, which he describes as not theoretically fundamental, is based on money illusion and money wage rigidity, and can be regarded as an objection to the specific way in which the effects of collective bargaining have been incorporated into the classical analysis; the second one, which he regards as theoretically fundamental, is an objection to the market-clearing theory of the labour market itself. It is argued that the labour market, in contrast to other markets, may not be stable and hence the assumption that it clears may not be justified. The argument is that when the labour market fails to clear, it will be the money wage which adjusts (if anything adjusts) and this may not induce the movement of the real wage appropriate to restore equilibrium. So the adjustment of the labour market in disequilibrium may not be equilibrating, and hence the assumption that the labour market clears may not be justified. This justifies constructing a theory of the workings of an economy where the labour market does not or need not clear, and when this theory has been constructed, the effects of money wage changes on employment can be considered. This is basically what the General Theory sets out to do.

In chapter 3, Keynes's analysis of the other prop of the classical system, Say's Law, is discussed. Keynes argues against Say's Law, and presents a framework, that of the aggregate demand and supply curves, whereby the level of output and employment can be determined. Say's Law is argued to entail that the curves should have specific shapes, which we have no *a priori* reason to assume that they should have. The bulk of the remainder of Keynes's book is devoted to analysing the factors underlying these curves in more depth.

In chapter 4, the components of the aggregate demand curve, consumption and investment, are analysed. Keynes's reason for stressing the dependence of consumption on income is argued to hinge upon the fact that the labour market may not clear and hence that the actual quantity of labour supplied constitutes an independent argument of the consumption function; this is basically Clower's rationale for the consumption function and makes it clear why the consumption function was seen to be an innovation in Keynes. Investment is argued to depend upon the interest rate; expectations are discussed, but this is a discussion of the specific form the investment function takes and is not a crucial part of the theory.

Chapter 5 discusses the role of money, uncertainty and the rate of interest in Keynesian economics. The classical theory of the rate of interest is argued to be incompatible with the aggregate demand/supply framework which Keynes has constructed, and hence a new theory of the rate of interest is required. This involves a money demand function which is to some extent dependent on the interest rate, and the theory of liquidity preference is introduced in order to justify such an interest dependent demand for money function. Uncertainty plays an important role in underpinning the speculative theory of the demand for money, and it is only here that uncertainty plays a crucial role in Keynesian economics. Keynes also presents some more speculative thoughts on the role of money in the economy and the nature of a monetary economy. His discussion is not entirely clear, but he emphasizes factors such as the fact that money is a non-reproducible store of value. There are other views on both money and uncertainty in the literature; in particular, there is the view that money is important in Keynesian economics inasmuch as it is the medium of exchange and the view which lays great stress on the role of uncertainty in Keynes's thought. Both these positions will be criticized, and some of the recent literature in the area will be discussed.

Chapter 6 discusses the effects of wage rate changes on output and employment. Only with the construction of a complete theory of the workings of the economy with a non-clearing labour market can the effects of money wage rate changes on output and employment be analysed. Keynes's conclusion is that a flexible wage rate policy is not likely to be very successful in raising output and employment, and even if it is successful, then a money supply policy could achieve the same ends more easily. Keynes may justly be criticized for ignoring the Pigou effect; however, the consequences of this omission are by no means as serious for Keynesian economics as is sometimes made out. It is argued that recognition of the Pigou effect changes a conclusion which is sometimes reached using Keynesian theory, but does not invalidate the theory itself.

In chapter 7 the relationship of the General Theory to Keynes's other works is discussed. The *Tract on Monetary Reform* and the *Treatise on Money* are the main works discussed and the development of Keynes's thought is traced.

Chapter 8 is largely a concluding chapter, where the interpretation presented here is summarized and contrasted with other interpretations; points of divergence are emphasized. The book concludes with a discussion of the relevance of Keynesian economics for today.

Perhaps it might be desirable to consider the often discussed question of whether Keynesian economics is equilibrium economics or not. This, it will be argued, is largely a semantic question. An equilibrium, as the concept will be used here, is a state of affairs where all the equations which constitute a model or theory are mutually satisfied.

To talk of a state of affairs as being an equilibrium is therefore to have in mind, if only implicitly, some theory. For example, a state of involuntary unemployment generated by a Keynesian model might be described as an equilibrium. However, it can also be described as a disequilibrium, where the implicit reference might be to any model which involves the labour market's clearing. Since models where all markets clear have a powerful hold on economists' imaginations, we might use the term 'disequilibrium economics' to refer to the analysis of models where not all markets are assumed to clear; nevertheless this does not prevent discussion of the equilibria such models generate. Hence the same state of affairs can be referred to both as an equilibrium and as a disequilibrium. But, to avoid the confusion which the use of these terms is likely to give, the author will try to avoid using them where this is possible.

Sometimes it has been argued that it is wrong to assume that there must be one coherent viewpoint in the General Theory. Consider the following passage: 'Patinkin somewhere condemns the *a priori* attribution of consistency to an author: it is a fallacy to take for granted that all the different passages in an author's work hang together comfortably and are consistent with a single coherent doctrine' (Yeager, 1973, p. 151). One certainly should not start off with an assumption of consistency; whether a work is reasonably consistent or not is surely something one should decide after having studied it; but it has struck the author for some time that the General Theory is fairly coherent and consistent (this is not to deny that there are mistakes in it) and that it is fairly clear what Keynes is trying to do in the book. One of the main purposes of this book is, indeed, to give an account of how Keynes's book can be interpreted as presenting a reasonably coherent doctrine.

Finally, perhaps we might ponder another passage from Yeager's article where he states that 'On reading Clower and Leijonhufvud's interpretations of Keynes I was struck by how much of their work is a positive contribution and how little of it is an exposition of what Keynes himself said or can reasonably be interpreted to have meant. They cite remarkably little chapter and verse in support of their interpretations' (*ibid.* p. 156).

This book will be somewhat different; it is intended to provide an interpretation of the General Theory and hence Keynes's work will be cited and referred to frequently; but the author feels that this is necessary in a work of this type and it is not something for which an apology is offered.

2   The Labour Market

Keynes discusses the labour market primarily in chapter 2 of his *General Theory*, although the appendix to chapter 19 also contains some relevant material. His chapter 2 will be discussed at some length for two main reasons: its interpretation plays an important role in the interpretation of Keynes presented here, and there seem to be several conflicting, yet unresolved views on it in the literature. This chapter is divided into two sections; in the first, an interpretation of Keynes's views on the labour market will be given, and in the second, other interpretations of his views on these matters will be discussed.

PART I

Keynes states the so-called classical theory of the labour market in the first few pages of his chapter. He makes it depend on two postulates, which together entail that the economy is at full employment equilibrium.

The first postulate is: 'The wage is equal to the marginal product of labour' (G.T., p.5), which under perfect competition amounts to postulating that the economy is on its labour demand curve.

The second postulate is: 'The utility of the wage[1] when a given volume of labour is employed is equal to the marginal disutility of that amount of employment' (G.T., p.5). This amounts to postulating that the economy is on its labour supply curve; combining the two postulates, we obtain the result that there is equilibrium in the labour market; the real wage is such that the quantity of labour which workers wish to supply at that real wage is equal to the quantity which employers want to demand. There is hence full employment and no involuntary unemployment, although it is stressed that the second classical postulate is compatible with 'frictional' unemployment and also with 'voluntary' unemployment, where the latter category is interpreted widely. In particular, it includes 'unemployment due to the refusal of a unit of labour, as a result of legislation or social practices or of combination for collective bargaining . . . to accept a reward corresponding to the value of the product attributable to its marginal productivity' (G.T., p. 6). Hence trade unions may be responsible for unemployment if they succeed in raising their members' wage rates above the equilibrium level but the resultant unemployment is to be classed as voluntary. Indeed, when Keynes proceeds to discuss the attitude of the classical economists to the unemployment of the recession, he states that it is this interpretation of the high contemporary rates of unemployment that they give. They admit that more labour would, as a rule, be forthcoming at the existing money-wage if it were demanded (G.T., p. 7), but reconcile this fact with their views on unemployment by postulating that this situation is due to 'an open or tacit agreement amongst workers not to work for less, and that if labour as a whole would agree to a reduction of money-wages, more employment would be forthcoming' (G.T., p. 8). Hence we have a theory of employment whereby all unemployment appearing to be involuntary is classed as voluntary due to the effects of open or tacit collusion. Such is the 'classical' theory of unemployment, and it is illustrated in Figs. 2.1(a) and 2.1(b).

In Fig. 2.1(a) the level of employment is determined by the intersection of the supply and demand curves for labour; Fig. 2.1(b) shows how the effects of collective bargaining might be incorporated into the analysis. Labour 'stipulates' a minimum real wage $(w/p)'$ and as a consequence employment is only N_1. The dotted lines $S'S'$ shows what the labour supply curve would be in the absence of collective bargaining; in this situation, there would be a level of employment N_2, higher than N_1. At the real wage rate $(w/p)'$ there appears to be excess supply of labour of an amount N_3-N_1, this being the amount employment could be increased at the given real wage rate by a rightward movement of

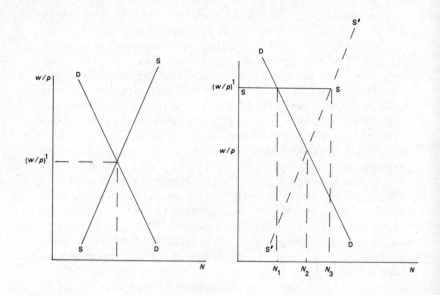

FIGURE 2.1(a)   FIGURE 2.1(b)

the demand curve. So collective bargaining is analysed as changing the labour supply curve from S'S' to S'SS.

It must be emphasized that this is the classical view of unemployment which Keynes is attacking. He attacks this theory for two reasons. It is important to note that the first reason he gives 'relates to the actual attitude of workers towards real wages and money-wages, respectively, and it is not theoretically fundamental' (G.T., p.8). It is basically an attack on the way in which the effects of collective bargaining are incorporated into the analysis as depicted in Fig. 2.1(b). It is this reason which is often described by statements such as 'Keynes assumed that workers suffer from money illusion' or 'Keynes assumed money-wage rigidity', but his reasoning is more subtle than is often suggested and it needs careful analysis.

Keynes suggests that experience tells us that the demand of labour is for a minimum money-wage and not for a minimum real wage, and this makes the classical analysis indeterminate. There are two questions to be discussed here; first, the implications that the fact that the labour force might behave in this way have for the analysis of the labour market and, secondly, the reasons why they might in fact behave in this way.

If workers behave as Keynes suggests they do, then it means that the supply of labour becomes a function of both the money and the real wage. Hence the partial equilibrium analysis of Fig. 2.1 is insufficient to determine the equilibrium level of employment, for 'the supply curve for labour will shift bodily with every movement of prices' (G.T., p. 9). This is illustrated in Fig. 2.2.

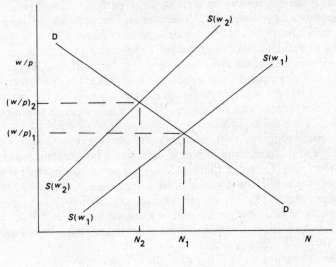

FIGURE 2.2

Here $S(w_1)$ is the supply curve of labour when the money wage is w_1 and $S(w_2)$ is the supply curve when the money-wage is w_2 (an infinite number of such curves could be drawn). The single labour market equilibrium condition is not sufficient to determine the quantity of employment uniquely, for there are two unknowns, the money-wage and the real wage, which need to be known before the equilibrium quantity of employment can be determined. Hence other factors need to be brought in if the quantity of employment is to be determined. (There is in fact no difficulty in doing this — once the full classical system is written down in equational form with the one modification that labour supply is a function of the money-wage as well as of the real wage, the system becomes determinate; so Keynes's first argument against the classical theory is invalid and it is fortunate he laid no theoretical weight on it; however, it is intended here to expound Keynes, not to criticize him). It must be emphasized that this argument of Keynes's, which is based on an apparent 'money illusion' on the part of workers, has a strictly subsidiary role in the General Theory and must not be used as the basis of an argument that Keynes assumed 'money illusion' in constructing his theory.

The second question to be discussed is that of explaining why workers should behave in such an apparently irrational fashion. Economists have dubbed such behaviour 'money illusion' and it can easily be shown that such behaviour is incompatible with 'a series of fundamental assumptions concerning the behaviour of individuals and business firms' (Leontief, 1936). Keynes suggests that this behaviour 'might not be so illogical as it appears at first' (G.T., p.9). An interpretation of Keynes's views on the matter will be presented and the approach taken here will be similar to that of Trevithick (1976).

Keynes suggests that workers are concerned about their relative real income and organize themselves into unions in order to protect it. They are therefore not prepared to see their own money-wage fall, for it would mean a decline in their relative real income. Attempts by employers to cut money-wages in a recession would tend to be met with withdrawal of labour by workers and this will impart a considerable amount of downward rigidity to the money-wage.

The situation arises because threatened money-wage reductions do not affect the whole labour force uniformly, but affect specific groups, who, perceiving a threat to their relative real income, resist such wage reductions. So workers, being concerned about their relative real incomes, act in such a manner as to impart a considerable amount of rigidity to the money-wage, and their behaviour can be represented by a labour supply function where labour supply is highly or perfectly elastic at the current money-wage. It appears that there is both money illusion in the labour supply function and downward money-wage rigidity; the labour supply function has the money-wage rate as an independent argument — this is one way of characterizing money illusion in supply or demand functions — and the fact that labour supply is highly elastic at the current money-wage gives rise to money-wage rigidity.

Hence one can say that 'money illusion' is a necessary part of the explanation Keynes gives for money-wage rigidity, but it is by no means sufficient. Of course, in general, money illusion and wage rigidity are quite distinct; Keynes's argument is a neat way of linking the two. So the inclusion of purely monetary values in the labour supply function need not imply irrational behaviour on the part of labour; it can be argued that it is a way of representing rational behaviour on the part of the labour force, where relative incomes affect utility; since money-wage changes are never uniform, it does not imply that workers suffer from the irrational type of money illusion which appears, or rather is rejected, in preference analysis. (More recent research has uncovered further reasons why labour supply might depend on prices independently of the real wage. First, the money-wage might have some informational content. For example, if expectations of wages obtainable elsewhere are fairly inelastic, then movements of the money-wages may be associated with changes in expected relative wages and hence may affect labour supply behaviour. Secondly, changes in the price level may be associated with changes in real wealth and labour supply may rationally depend upon this, as in, for example, Barro-Grossman (1976) p. 18).

This then is Keynes's first objection to the classical theory of employment. So, to summarize, the objection is that the way in which the effects of collective bargaining have been incorporated into the classical analysis is deficient; if the demand of labour is for a minimum money-wage, and not for a minimum real wage, as is argued to be likely, then the classical theory may be unable to deal with it. He adds on the further consideration that it does not seem empirically plausible that recessions are due to labour's demanding too much, either in money or in real terms — 'Wide variations are experienced in the volume of employment without any apparent change either in the minimum real demands of labour or in its productivity. Labour is not more truculent in the depression than in the boom — far from it' (G.T., p. 9). So, empirically, the suggestion that the unemployment of the Depression was due to excessive real demands on the part of the labour force does not seem particularly plausible.

Keynes's second objection to the classical theory of employment, which he regards as 'theoretically fundamental', relates to the equilibrium theory of employment as depicted in Fig. 2.1(a), whereas the first objection related to the specific way in which collective bargaining was introduced into the analysis, as illustrated in Fig. 2.1(b). The objection is that 'there may be no method available to labour as a whole whereby it can bring the wage-goods equivalent of the general level of money-wages into conformity with the marginal disutility of the current volume of employment' (G.T., p. 13). The argument embodied in this somewhat cryptic statement plays an important part in the interpretation advanced in this book, and will, therefore, be discussed at some length.

The classical theory of the labour market postulates that the labour market clears. It is by no means clear that this assumption is justified. Indeed, fictive devices (such as the auctioneer or recontracting) have sometimes been introduced in order to justify the assumption that markets always clear. Nevertheless, many economists might accept a justification of equilibrium analysis which goes somewhat as follows: equilibrium analysis may be a useful tool of economic analysis when we can be sure that the relevant market or markets are stable. For example, in Fig. 2.3 there is a unique equilibrium at price p_1 and quantity q_1; we might ask, however, what will happen if the economy is not in equilibrium? A reasonable assumption is that there would be some sort

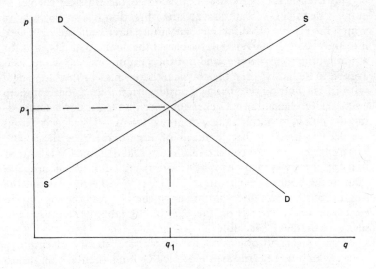

FIGURE 2.3

of adjustment. For example, if the price is above the equilibrium price, then since the quantity suppliers will wish to supply exceeds the quantity demanders wish to demand, we would expect the price to be bid down, and similarly we would expect the price to be bid up if the price is below the equilibrium one. Provided this process takes place reasonably quickly, we would expect that, over time, as long as the supply and demand curves remain fairly steady, the price will come to approximate the equilibrium price. Hence if we know that the market is stable, equilibrium analysis may tell us a lot about the behaviour of the market. It is clear that prices do not change instantaneously when demand or supply curves shift, and therefore there must be some moments of disequilibrium. Nevertheless, it would be argued, such disequilibria would be limited in extent and essentially short-lived, so that equilibrium analysis could provide a useful approximation to the behaviour of the market and provide valuable insights. Hence, if we are guaranteed stability, there is a strong case for using equilibrium analysis. It seems to follow that if the supply and demand curves have the right shape to justify stability (and this is a fairly weak requirement for most plausible price adjustment mechanisms), then persistent disequilibrium can only occur if prices do not or cannot move towards their equilibrium values. This is perhaps one of the reasons why 'wage rigidity' is an argument commonly given for the persistence of unemployment (that is, non-market clearing) in the labour market. In fact, it sometimes seems difficult to think of any other reason why a market should persistently fail to clear. Nevertheless, there is another reason which can be given, and it is this reason which Keynes gives as his 'fundamental objection' to the classical theory of employment.

In the analysis of the market depicted in Fig. 2.3 it is the price of the commodity which is an argument of the supply and demand curves for that commodity and similarly it is that price which adjusts when the market does not clear. However, this need not be so; the variable which adjusts in such circumstances need not be the variable which enters as an argument into the supply and demand curves. If this is so, then we have another reason why a market may persistently fail to clear. An example is provided by the labour market. It is the real wage which is an argument of the labour supply and demand functions, but it is the money-wage which adjusts (if anything adjusts) in disequilibrium; for equilibrium to be restored, there must be an adjustment of the real wage. Will this happen? Keynes presents an argument which suggests that, on classical assumptions, it might not. He suggests that a fall in the money-wage will lead to a reduction in the marginal prime costs facing entrepreneurs and hence to a reduction in their prices. So 'prices would change in almost the same proportion, leaving the real wage and the level of unemployment practically the same as before' (G.T., p.12). Money-wage changes may not lead to an appropriate adjustment of the real wage — money-wage changes may not be equilibrating. Hence, the assumption that the labour market clears may not be justifiable and analysis which is based upon the assumption that it does may well be extremely misleading. One might therefore be justified in asking what does happen in the labour market, given that it may not clear. (One might also ask what consequences this might have for the rest of the economy.) At the time that Keynes was writing the General Theory, it was impossible to answer this question; there was no theory of the workings of an economy with a non-clearing labour market. It was therefore necessary to construct such a theory; this would, among other things, enable the effect money-wage changes might have on output to be analysed. As Keynes says, we need 'to throw over the second postulate of the classical doctrine and to work out the behaviour of a system in which involuntary unemployment in the strict sense is possible' (G.T., pp.16-17). And it is this that the General Theory tries to do.

This, then, is Keynes's 'fundamental objection' to the classical theory of employment. It is not based in any way on an assumption of wage rigidity or money illusion. It is that the labour market — in contrast to other markets — may not be stable and therefore the assumption that it clears may not be justified. In order to find out what does happen in the labour market, and the conditions under which money-wages changes in the labour market might be equilibrating, a theory of the workings of the economy when the labour market may not clear was required; a theory which Keynes proceeded to construct.

It is important to avoid misconceptions on this question. The argument is not that prices will change to exactly the same extent as money-wages, hence keeping real wages constant. The argument is rather the much weaker one that money-wage adjustments may not produce the adjustment in the real wage required to restore full-employment equilibrium.

Moreover, it is important to distinguish the argument presented in chapter 2 from the more detailed arguments concerning money-wage changes in chapter 19. The former constitutes Keynes's principal objection to the classical theory of employment, whilst the latter constitute Keynes's application of his own theory to analyse the question of what effect money-wage changes will actually have on employment, and hence the real wage — a question with which he claimed the classical theory was unable to cope.

Before going on to consider other writers' interpretations of chapter 2, there are several further questions which arise which might be appropriate to discuss here.

It is perhaps important to note that Keynes considers the possibility that it might be up to labour to change its money-wage rate : 'there may be no method available to labour as a whole . . .' (G.T., p. 13). This does not mean that he actually believed that it was labour which was responsible for determining or changing its wage-rate, but that his argument was that *even if* labour could determine its own money-wage, it still might not be able to bring about the appropriate change in the real wage rate. In general, Keynes considers that prices are made by the market participants — he talks of 'the wage bargains between the entrepreneurs and the workers' (G.T., p. 11) — he does not introduce any fictive device such as an 'auctioneer' and he does not consider that his failure to do so is in any way revolutionary. This is a point which perhaps ought to be borne in mind when we come to consider Leijonhufvud's contention that the major innovation in Keynes was his removal of the Walrasian auctioneer and the associated tâtonnement mechanism. The importance of the point that Keynes assumed that prices were adjusted in this way is perhaps that it has disguised the fact that in pages 11-13 of the General Theory, Keynes is in fact discussing the behaviour of the labour market in disequilibrium; he does not assume, for example, that prices move automatically in response to the discrepancy between supply and demand. But although he assumes a different kind of adjustment mechanism, it seems fairly clear that he is discussing the disequilibrium behaviour of the labour market; to repeat: 'there may exist no expedient by which labour as a whole can reduce its real wage to a given figure by making revised money bargains with the entrepreneurs' (G.T., p. 13). In other words, changes in money-wage rates would not, or might not, produce the requisite adjustment of the real wage. Keynes here is not asserting money-wage rigidity, for he is discussing the implications of changes in money-wage rates.

It is interesting to contrast Keynes's explanation of the contemporary unemployment with the classical explanation. According to the classics, a large amount of unemployment was due to labour's refusing to accept a reward appropriate to its full employment marginal product, without its being doubted that a reduction in money-wages might lead to a more appropriate reward. Keynes's interpretation of the unemployment is different; labour may be prepared to accept a lower reward, in both money and real terms, but in making revised money bargains it may not in fact achieve the appropriate lowering of the reward in real terms. So the classics believed that there was a mechanism whereby the labour force could ensure that it received a reward appropriate to its full employment marginal product. Keynes disagreed; he thought that there might not be, and analysis of whether in fact adjustment in the labour market would be equilibrating required the construction of a theory of the behaviour of an economy where it is possible for the labour market not to clear.

In the rest of the General Theory Keynes does this; he works out the economics of a system in which the labour market may not clear; hence factors other than the slope and intersection of the supply and demand schedules for labour determine the volume of employment. The assumption that the wage is equal to the value of the marginal product of labour, however, is retained (see G.T., p. 17) so firms are still assumed to be on their labour demand curves. In fact, in Keynesian economics, we are on that portion of the demand curve to the left of E in Fig. 2.4. Note that it has not been assumed that the labour supply and demand curves have any particular or peculiar shapes. According to the interpretation advanced here, Keynes's fundamental difference from the classics was one of relaxing the labour market clearing assumption, not one of making restrictive assumptions about the form of the supply and demand curves for labour.

Keynes did not consider the case of overfull employment, where the real wage is below $(w/p)^e$. So to this extent, Keynesian economics is the 'economics of depression'.

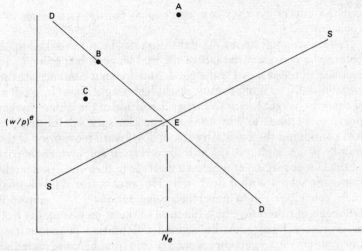

FIGURE 2.4

Keynes's definition of involuntary unemployment does perhaps merit some consideration. According to the definition 'men are involuntarily unemployed if, in the event of a small rise in the price of wage-goods relatively to the money-wage, both the aggregate supply of labour willing to work for the current wage rate and the aggregate demand for it at that wage would be greater than the existing volume of employment' (G.T., p.15). There are several things to note in this definition.

First, consider points A, B and C in the above diagram. From Keynes's definition of involuntary unemployment, points B and C are positions of involuntary unemployment, but point A is not; if employment and the real wage were as represented in A, then if there were a small downward movement in the real wage, the supply side criterion in the above definition would be met but the demand side criterion would not be; if the real wage falls slightly, due to an increase in the price level, then it is not true that 'the aggregate demand for it [that is, labour] at that wage would be greater than the existing volume of employment'. However, at A there does seem to be excess supply of labour, so Keynes's use of the term 'involuntary unemployment' does not correspond with our use of the term 'excess supply of labour'. This is perhaps just an academic consideration; points such as A will presumably not be observed in practice; as long as employers are on their labour demand curves, as they are assumed to be, the two terms are coextensive.

A second point about the definition has been remarked upon before; he considers the fall in the real wage as being due to an increase in the price of wage goods and does not contemplate the possibility that a similar result might be brought about by a fall in the money-wage. Keynes's earlier discussion of the labour market provides a clue as to why he should proffer such a definition. He had considered the possibility that a downward movement of the money-wage might cause a withdrawal from employment of part of the labour force, yet where an increase in the price level might not cause such a withdrawal, and gives reasons for thinking that such behaviour might nevertheless be rational. The supply of labour might therefore be a function of the money-wage, as well as of the real wage. As he wanted a definition of involuntary unemployment to encompass such a situation, he constructed an appropriate definition. So it is a definition which works well whether or not there is money illusion; it does not entail that Keynes assumed money-wage illusion, as is suggested in an argument cited by Leijonhufvud: 'The juxtaposition of these two arguments seems to lead to the unavoidable conclusion that Keynes' theory was based on the assumption of money illusion on the part of workers' (Leijonhufvud, 1968, pp. 94-5). But such a conclusion is avoidable; to allow for a possibility is not to make it a fundamental assumption of the analysis. Leijonhufvud himself rejects this argument for a reason which the author finds incomprehensible (*ibid.*, p. 95).

A third point to note on this definition is that it is intended as a criterion for the presence of involuntary unemployment in the economy (although how operational this criterion is, is debateable, since it requires a *ceteris paribus* fall in the real wage!). It is not intended as a criterion for assessing whether any particular person is involuntarily unemployed or not.

Keynes also discusses Say's Law in the chapter in which he discusses the labour market; consideration of this will be postponed until the next chapter where its relationship with the concepts of aggregate demand and supply will hopefully become clearer. This concludes the discussion of Keynes's views on the labour market and the part these play in the structure of his theory. In the second section of this chapter, some other writers' views on Keynes and the labour market will be considered.

PART II

What might be called the standard interpretation of Keynes's views on the labour market is that Keynes assumed that money wages were rigid, or at least sticky (sometimes it is asserted that it is *downward* money-wage rigidity which is the crucial assumption; this distinction will not be important in the discussion to follow). For example:

(i) 'Keynesian theory [can explain] the consistency of economic equilibrium with the presence of involuntary unemployment. It is, however, not sufficiently recognised ... this result is due entirely to the assumption of "rigid wages" and not to the Keynesian liquidity preference' (Modigliani, 1944, p. 65).
(ii) 'Keynes assumed that wages were rigid downwards because workers are subject to a "money illusion"' (Blaug, 1968, p. 645).
(iii) '... speculation in security markets, allied to money wage stickiness, may interfere with a full employment temporary equilibrium that might otherwise be attained' (Bliss, 1975, p. 213).

This view is attractive for a number of reasons. First, it seems difficult to think of any other reason why a market could persistently fail to clear. Secondly, it seems a fairly natural interpretation of chapter 2 of the General Theory. And thirdly, discussion of the Pigou effect seems to have shown fairly decisively that a permanent underemployment state is impossible if wages are flexible. An alternative view is that Keynes thought he had established the possibility of an underemployment equilibrium with flexible prices, but that subsequent discussion of the Pigou effect has shown that this is wrong — this is the line taken by Friedman for example (see Friedman, 1974, pp. 15-6). Nevertheless, it will be argued here that such an interpretation is wrong.

It seems clear, and this has been pointed out before, that Keynes does not assume that money-wages are rigid downwards. For example, chapter 19 is entitled 'Changes in Money-Wages' and in this chapter he considers the effect changes in money-wages have on output and employment; this is hardly compatible with an assumption of downward rigid money-wages. In giving a summary of his theory of employment in chapter 3, he writes:

In this summary we shall assume that the money-wage and other factor costs are constant per unit of labour employed. But this simplification, with which we shall dispense later, is introduced solely to facilitate the exposition. The essential character of the argument is precisely the same whether or not money-wages, etc., are liable to change (G.T., p.27).

Patinkin writes: 'Thus wage rigidities . . . are not an assumption of the analysis, but the policy conclusion which Keynes reaches after investigating the results to be expected from wage flexibility' (Patinkin, 1965, p.643).

So there seems to be some quite clear textual evidence that Keynes did not assume money-rigidity. Moreover, it will be argued, none of the reasons given earlier for thinking this interpretation of Keynes attractive is at all compelling.

The Pigou effect and its implications will be discussed later in chapter 6. To summarize the argument to be presented there, it will be argued that the Pigou effect is something which ought to be considered when the Keynesian System is used to analyse the *consequences* of money-wage changes; it hence does not seem to provide a good reason for asserting that Keynes either did assume or ought to have assumed money-wage rigidity. The first reason why money-wage rigidity is perhaps an attractive interpretation of Keynes has been answered, at least implicitly, above. There is an alternative reason why a market might persistently fail to clear — the market may adjust, but the adjustment may fail to be equilibrating; as emphasized before, it is this which Keynes considers to be the 'theoretically fundamental' objection to the classical theory of employment. We have answered the second reason given above by providing an alternative explanation of chapter 2 of the General Theory, where Keynes is not arguing for an assumption of money-wage rigidity.

So we are led to reject the money-wage rigidity interpretation of Keynes. Instead, we might characterize his position in the following way. He presents an argument which has nothing to do with money-wage rigidity for relaxing the labour market clearing assumption. In order to prevent the system from becoming underdetermined, an exogenous money-wage rate is assumed. This is not explicit in Keynes, but it seems fairly clear that Keynes had no explicit theory of how the money-wage rate, or its rate of change, is determined: 'It is hard to see that in his book he has *any* theory about the causation of changes in money-wages' (Hicks, 1974, p.61). So the equational representation of the Keynesian system is the same as that propounded by those who interpret Keynes as assuming money-wage rigidity, but the interpretation here is that instead of assuming money-wage rigidity, and *therefore* relaxing the labour market clearing assumption, he instead relaxed the labour market clearing assumption (for other reasons) and *therefore* assumed an exogenous money-wage. This is the only modification Keynes made to the classical system as represented by the six equations in chapter 1 of this book, although with the modification made, the interpretation of some of the other components of the system changes, as will be discussed later in this book.

We now turn to a consideration of Leijonhufvud's approach to Keynes's discussion of the labour market. His views on whether Keynes assumed that labour supply behaviour was characterized by money illusion have already been discussed. The main topic which will be discussed here will be his discussion of wage rigidity and unemployment; also, some consideration will be given to his discussion of Keynes's objections to the classical postulates.

Leijonhufvud is somewhat vague on the reasons why unemployed resources might emerge. He does discuss search theory[2] and search unemployment, but it does not seem that he uses this to explain involuntary unemployment; rather it is used to explain wage and price inflexibility. His account of why prices are relatively sticky when the economy suffers a deflationary shock goes somewhat as follows: there is a fall in aggregate demand and employers would like to cut money-wages; some of them do. Workers employed in the industries where wages have fallen have inelastic expectations about the wages they might obtain elsewhere in the economy. They therefore quit and search for other jobs. Therefore the extent to which wages fall in these industries is limited. So we have an explanation, not for complete downward wage rigidity — indeed the process relies on some wage cuts actually being implemented — but for a high degree of wage inflexibility. Indeed, it might be neatly characterized by the statement that workers have a speculative demand for their own labour services. The essence of the approach is that it is lack of information, rather than monopolistic collusion which is responsible for a high degree of money-wage inflexibility. It is not my purpose here to offer a detailed critique of 'search theory'; however, one should note that the above account is based on a number of restrictive assumptions. It is assumed that search is done more efficiently when unemployed and the assumption that workers have inelastic expectations about job opportunities and wages obtainable elsewhere is restrictive and does not seem to have been justified. Moreover, movements in unemployment are assumed to take place through changes in quit rates rather than through layoffs. An attempt has been made to explain layoffs using search theory by Alchian; the explanation goes as follows: suppose firms do cut wages; then they know from experience that a large number of workers will quit in order to search for better jobs; instead of going through the tedious process of cutting money-wages and seeing their work force gradually decline, it is much more convenient for them to lay off a certain proportion of the work force (see Alchian, 1969, p. 118). However, as Barro and Grossman point out (see Barro and Grossman, 1976, p. 249), this explanation does not work; the firm will not be optimizing if it cuts employment without cutting wages; what it should do, presumably, is cut both employment and wages. Moreover, the idea that there could be a speculative demand for labour services is really absurd. A speculative demand must be for a storable commodity; the very idea of speculation is that by selling the goods later it is possible to make a profit. But labour services are normally regarded as a pure flow and hence non-storable. The idea that a speculative demand for labour could exist is hence rather perverse. Much research has been done in the area, but the precise implications of informational deficiencies (less than perfect information) for price movements and unemployment are not yet entirely clear. However, let us assume that the account given above of how unemployed resources emerge is broadly correct and examine its implications.

The important question is whether such an account provides an adequate underpinning for Keynesian economics; it will be argued here that it does not. The first point to note is that the movements in unemployment which it explains are entirely movements in voluntary unemployment, in the sense that labour remains on its supply curve. No reason is given for labour's ever being off its supply curve. Hence we can conclude that the movements in unemployment which the theory explains are not the movements with which Keynes was fundamentally concerned, namely those of involuntary unemployment. But we must not be too hasty; it might be argued that although the theory does not explain Keynesian unemployment directly, it does explain money-wage rigidity, and it is this that is responsible for involuntary unemployment. However, the explanation again fails; the money-wage inflexibility which the theory explains is the product of both supply and demand factors in the labour market, and it is through the adjustment of supply that the money-wage is kept (approximately) constant. The normal way in which wage inflexibility is regarded as being responsible for involuntary unemployment is quite different; the inflexibility of the money-wage is given or imposed from outside and is seen to have certain consequences for the labour market. So here, involuntary unemployment becomes possible if the condition that labour must be on its supply curve is relaxed. However, it is impossible to confront labour with an inflexible money-wage in the search theoretic case and examine its consequences for equilibrium in the labour market, for the outcome is already a consequence of equilibrium in the labour market. Hence, it seems impossible to use the theory in this way to underpin Keynesian economics. However, the theory can perhaps be used to complement a theory of involuntary unemployment; the theory could help explain why wages might not fall extensively when involuntary unemployment emerges, but it needs to be linked to a different theory of why the labour market might not clear in the first place. It is this approach which Leijonhufvud adopts:

Alchian's analysis remains perfectly applicable to the explanation of individual behaviour in a state of 'involuntary' unemployment, and the initial 'inflexibility' of reservation prices that his analysis implies is, indeed, a necessary condition for the emergence of such a state. But it is not sufficient. Keynes's involuntary unemployment is fundamentally a product of the cumulative process which he assumed the initial increase in unemployment would trigger (Leijonhufvud, 1968, p. 81).

So, it being common ground that search theory on its own cannot explain non-clearing in the labour market, the next task is to examine what further reasons might be given for thinking that the labour market might not clear. Leijonhufvud seems rather unclear why this might happen. The only reason I can find in Leijonhufvud which might complement imperfect information as an explanation for involuntary unemployment is to do with money's role as a medium of exchange. The assertion is made that 'the dynamic properties of an economic system depend upon what I will call its "transaction structure"' (*ibid.*, p. 90) and an argument is produced to support this; the argument goes somewhat as follows — in a barter economy, where goods exchange for goods, involuntary unemployment will not occur; if there were involuntary unemployment, workers and firms could indulge in a mutually beneficial swap of work for goods, an offer to work by an unemployed worker constitutes 'effective demand'[3] for output and the unemployed worker will be employed. However, in a monetary economy, this will not occur; the offer by the worker does not constitute 'effective demand for output' (because it is money, not output, which is demanded in exchange for labour) and hence the worker will not be employed, even though he would be prepared to work for a wage less than the value of his marginal product. The argument is fallacious; the firm will have exactly the same incentive to employ the worker in both cases. In the latter case, the firm can sell the extra output produced by the additional worker if it is prepared to lower its price; the firm should therefore compute the marginal value product of the worker and employ him if this is greater than the wage; but it is exactly the same criterion that the firm should use in the former case. The worker will presumably barter the goods he receives in order to live; this may mean that the price of the goods produced by the firm is reduced; presumably, if the firm is rational, it should take this effect into account as well and employ the worker if his marginal value product is greater than the wage. Hence this argument that money as a medium of exchange is responsible for disequilibrium is fallacious. Hahn (1977) argues for the same conclusion: 'it is a muddle to suppose that in the absence of this axiomatic restriction [that is, that "money buys goods"] things would be different' (p. 31). Grossman (1974), however, argues for a different conclusion — this argument will be considered in a later chapter.

So, to sum up on Leijonhufvud's reasons for thinking that involuntary unemployment is possible: 'search theory' on its own may explain wage and price stickiness but not involuntary unemployment; it might be used to complement other reasons for involuntary unemployment, which, however, Leijonhufvud fails to give, his argument based on the transactions structure of the economy being incorrect.

Finally, we come to Leijonhufvud's discussion of Keynes's objections to the classical theory of employment.

When Leijonhufvud discusses Keynes's first objection to the classical theory of employment, he interprets Keynes as putting over what is basically a search theoretic account of wage rigidity. But there is little support for this interpretation in the text. Keynes is discussing the role of collusion on the part of the workers and how it should be analysed, and suggests that if workers stipulated for a minimum money-wage, as opposed to a minimum real wage, the outcome cannot be analysed using the classical framework. The analysis underlying this refers to the collective behaviour of workers within an industry — it does not refer to the possibility of workers becoming unemployed in order to search for better jobs. There is no evidence here that when Keynes talks about workers resisting wage cuts, he is referring to their quitting and searching. A much more natural interpretation is that he is referring to their actions within their own industries (for example, industrial action).

However, there is one passage later in the book, where Keynes seems to hint at the possibility of a search theoretic type explanation for money-wage rigidity. Consider the following passage: 'workers will not ... allow a very great reduction [in the money-wage] rather than suffer any unemployment at all' (G.T., p. 253).

Leijonhufvud then goes on to outline Keynes's 'theoretically fundamental' reason for rejecting the classical theory of employment as he sees it:

the fact that there exists a potential barter bargain of goods for labour services that would be mutually agreeable to producers as a group and labour as a group is irrelevant to the motion of the system. In economies relying on a means of payment, the excess demand for wage goods corresponding to an excess supply of labour is but 'notional' — it is not communicated to employers as effective demand for output. The resulting miseries are 'involuntary' all around (Leijonhufvud, 1968, p. 98).

There are basically two points to make about such an argument. First, the question of the implications of disequilibrium is confused with the question of its existence. It is an implication of disequilibrium that notional and effective demands will differ, but the fact that an excess demand for wage goods may correspond to an excess supply of labour tells us nothing about the motion of the system — in either the barter or the money case. Secondly,

Keynes, in his argument against the classical school, does not mention effective demand for wage-goods; his concern is rather whether the appropriate adjustment of the real wage will be induced; this is, as we have already argued, the crucial point in Keynes.

This concludes the discussion of Leijonhufvud's interpretation of Keynes's analysis of the labour market. Other aspects of his interpretation will be discussed later in this book.

Hahn and Leontief refer explicitly to Keynes's discussion in chapter 2 as one of homogeneity, presumably in the labour supply function. According to Leontief, Keynes's fundamental postulate is his denial that the labour supply function is homogenous of degree zero in all prices and (money-) wages (that is, that an equi-proportionate change in all wages and prices will leave the quantity of labour supplied unchanged). This is equivalent to saying that the labour force suffers from money illusion, an interpretation which has already been discussed in this chapter. Again, the appropriate response is that although Keynes may have believed in money illusion, he did not assume it; and it has been argued that the fundamental assumption of Keynes's theory was quite different. Hahn writes: 'Keynes's own discussion of the consequences of the wage bargain being in money terms only makes sense as a discussion of homogeneity and in any case it was not, as given in that chapter, correct' (Hahn, 1977, p. 38). This is a somewhat cryptic comment; one wishes he were more precise and would say precisely where Keynes is wrong. However, this interpretation is inconsistent with the interpretation given here; Keynes's discussion of the wage bargain's being in money terms is not a discussion of homogeneity; it is a discussion of the stability of the labour market; nor has an argument been produced to show that there is anything of importance in the chapter which is, at a theoretical level, wrong.

Malinvaud, in his Yrjo Jahnsson Lectures, introduces a supply and demand curve for labour, as in Fig. 2.1(a) and describes that theory as classical, which assumes that the wage rate will adjust until the labour market is cleared. He rejects the classical theory for the following reason: 'it neglects the fact that, in the situations actually observed, rationing in the labour market is related to and dependent on, rationing in the goods markets' (Malinvaud, 1977, p. 3). So for Malinvaud, it is the fact that more than one market will generally fail to clear that accounts for the fact that the equilibrium analysis of the labour market is inadequate; in order to know, for example, the level of employment we need to know not just the labour demand curve and the real wage, we also need to know the quantity of output which firms can sell and the production function.

Now this is certainly a reason why the equilibrium analysis of the labour market may be inadequate; however, it is important to note that this is not the reason Keynes gave. The Malinvaud approach relies on the possibility of other markets not clearing; in the General Theory, as has often been pointed out, (for example, Grossman, 1972, p. 28 fn. 11) it is just the labour market which, it is assumed, may not clear. Keynes emphasized that he is retaining the first postulate that the wage is equal to the marginal product of labour. This would not be the case if firms were rationed on the goods market; firms would want to supply more than they were constrained to supply; hence the marginal product of labour would be *above* the real wage. So in Keynes's economics there is no rationing on the goods market. It is not, therefore, the reason why the classical analysis is criticized in the General Theory. Malinvaud does not give Keynes's reason for rejecting the classical analysis — namely that adjustment in the labour market may not be equilibrating — indeed, he writes: 'whether nominal or real wage rate is considered does not matter at this stage' (Malinvaud, 1977, p. 2 fn. 2). However, the distinction between the money and the real wage rate was, as we have seen, of crucial importance in Keynes's argument against the classical theory of employment.

It has been argued that Keynes's fundamental objection to the classical analysis of the labour market concerned stability and on the basis of this he felt justified in constructing a theory of the workings of an economy with a non-clearing labour market. This does not seem to have been propounded before in the literature, although it does seem to have been discussed — and rejected — by Clower. Consider the following passage: 'the burden of his argument seems to be that if labour is ever forced to move "off its supply curve", it may be unable to get back on again' (Clower, 1965, p. 277). Hence he seems to suggest that *prima facie* Keynes is concerned with the stability analysis of the labour market. His reason for rejecting this interpretation, though, is not convincing; it is that 'there is no reason for thinking that Keynes was more expert at stability analysis than his orthodox predecessors' (*ibid.*) This seems to be nothing more than begging the question. If this interpretation of Keynes is correct, then this presumably is evidence that Keynes had at least some ability at stability analysis; if it is false, then presumably he did not. So in order to ascertain whether 'Keynes was more expert at stability analysis' etc., we need to know whether to interpret the General Theory as stability analysis. But in order to do that, we surely need some independent argument as to why or why not it should be so interpreted. This Clower does not produce. It is a major contention of the present work that the General Theory should, in fact, be analysed in this way. But there is no need to disparage Clower's contribution. He presents what he considers to be an alternative interpretation of the chapter, in which he introduces his ideas about the dual decision hypothesis and the role of income in the consumption function. (This will be discussed later.) It will be argued that this is relevant and important to our understanding of Keynesian economics; in particular, it provides a theoretical underpinning to the Keynesian consumption function. But the contribution is not relevant as an interpretation of Keynes's chapter 2; it is later, when Keynes discusses the consumption function, that his contribution becomes relevant. So one can retain the interpretation of chapter 2 presented here (which Clower rejects) with Clower's substantive contribution, interpreted as a theoretical rationale for the Keynesian consumption function.

Bliss is another writer who argues that Keynes's view of the labour market is different from his view of other markets: 'it does look as though the particular view which Keynes took of the operation of the labour market, which view was in sharp contrast to the neoclassical idea that factor markets are just like any other market subject to exactly the same laws of supply and demand, is a very essential component of his theory' (Bliss, 1975, p. 208). But Bliss seems to conclude that this means that Keynes assumed that money-wages were rigid, or at least sticky. The interpretation presented here concurs in picking out the labour market for special attention, but not in characterizing it as the market where price adjustments are slowest. Money wages may change quite quickly in the labour market, but what is relevant is that the right kind of adjustment in the labour market might not be induced.

The role of the rest of the General Theory now becomes

clearer. In order to work out exactly what effect money-wage changes do have on output and employment, it is necessary to construct a theory of an economy where the labour market need not clear: 'we need to throw over the second postulate of the classical doctrine and to work out the behaviour of a system in which involuntary unemployment in the strict sense is possible' (G.T., p.16-7). This is what the bulk of the General Theory is devoted to, and only when such a theory has been considered can the effects of money-wage changes be properly considered. In subsequent chapters an attempt will be made to explain how Keynes set about constructing his theory.

NOTES

1 It should be marginal utility of the wage — I take it that this is just a slip by Keynes, but one which, to my knowledge, has not hitherto been remarked upon.
2 By 'search theory' is meant a theory where the distribution of prices believed to be obtainable elsewhere either spatially or temporally, is an argument of supply or demand functions. For discussion of search theory, see Phelps (1970), Rothschild (1973), Lippman and McCall (1976).
3 The concept of 'effective demand' will be discussed more extensively in the next chapter.

3   Say's Law and Aggregate Demand and Supply Curves

Having discussed the labour market in the first five sections of chapter 2, Keynes proceeds to discuss Say's Law in the remainder of the chapter, although he does not actually describe it as such until chapter 3, where he introduces the concepts of aggregate supply and demand curves and interprets Say's Law within this framework. The discussion is not entirely clear and rather brief for such an important component of his theory. In this chapter an interpretation of Keynes's analysis will be given; attention will be focused on his rejection of Say's Law and his use of aggregate demand and supply curves.

Say's Law is often expressed by the statement 'Supply creates its own Demand', but was regarded by Keynes as equivalent to the proposition that 'there is no such thing as involuntary unemployment in the strict sense' (G.T., p. 21). It is by no means clear that the two propositions amount to the same thing; however, it seems clear that if Say's Law is to play the role it is normally assumed to play in classical theory, it must be interpreted in the latter sense; there is no involuntary unemployment — full employment equilibrium is continuously and automatically maintained via the working of the economic system. The statement 'Supply creates its own Demand' may perhaps better be regarded as an abbreviation of the argument underlying Say's Law, which rests on the interaction between supply and demand. It is not, however, an argument which is based on the behaviour of the labour market, as was the argument we have considered in the previous chapter; it is hence another argument that the full employment level of income will be maintained but one which concentrates on the market for commodities and not on the labour market. So if $\overline{N}$ is the level of full employment (the point where the demand and supply schedules for labour cross) then the full employment level of output is defined by $\overline{Y}$, where $\overline{Y} = f(\overline{N})$, $f(\quad)$ being the (short run) production function. So the classical argument based on the labour market concentrated on arguing that $\overline{N}$ would be continuously maintained; Say's Law holds that $\overline{Y}$ will continuously be maintained; hence we can see that Say's Law and the classical theory of the labour market 'amount to the same thing in the sense that they ... stand and fall together, [either] one of them logically involving the other ...' (G.T., p. 22).

This statement of Say's Law may appear somewhat unusual and has not, to my knowledge, appeared in the literature before; hence a discussion of the extent to which it is a justifiable statement of Say's Law would therefore seem necessary. There are basically two things to discuss here; first, whether it is equivalent to Say's Law as stated and attacked by Keynes, and secondly, whether it is equivalent to Say's Law as propounded by the classical economists.

As far as the first question is concerned, it seems fairly clear with one proviso that Say's Law as formulated above is equivalent to what Keynes regarded as Say's Law. As has been seen Keynes interpreted it to be equivalent to the proposition that there is no involuntary unemployment; according to the above formulation, $Y = \overline{Y}$ is both necessary and sufficient for full employment. When Keynes interprets Say's Law in terms of aggregate demand and supply curves, he argues that 'the classical theory assumes that the aggregate demand price always accommodates itself to the aggregate supply price; so that competition between entrepreneurs would always lead to an expansion of output up to the point at which the supply of output as a whole ceases to be elastic' (G.T., p. 26). So again, it seems to be equivalent to the proposition that there is continuous full employment, which is what is stated in the above formulation. The proviso is that it is not clear whether the dynamic mechanism whereby entrepreneurs are led to expand output and employment should be incorporated within the statement of Say's Law itself, so that Say's Law might just be stated as the proposition that every level of income is an equilibrium level of income, or that 'there is no obstacle to full employment' (G.T., p.26). However, since Keynes did seem to think that there would be this dynamic process which would generate full employment in this case, the difference is perhaps not important. So, with this proviso, Say's Law as stated above does seem to be equivalent to what Keynes regarded as Say's Law. As interpreted in this way, it can be regarded as a foundation to the classical theory alternative to that provided by the labour market equilibrium condition, and it can be seen how it fits into the classical system.

Previous discussions of Say's Law have often been rather vague on how it should be stated, reluctant to formalize it and disinclined to specify how it is related to the rest of the classical system. It is hoped that the foregoing discussion will enable at least these charges to be avoided.

The second question is whether Say's Law as stated above is equivalent to Say's Law as propounded by the classical economists. We must remember that 'There was no definitive statement of Say's Law in classical economics . . . . Nevertheless there was a solid core of propositions on which the whole orthodox tradition was agreed and a penumbra of corollaries and related ideas to which some subscribed and some did not' (Sowell, 1972, p.12). Sowell gives a list of seven propositions which Say's Law involved, (*ibid.*, pp.32-3) although when it is introduced it is described as 'The idea that supply creates its own demand' (*ibid.*, p.1). So although Keynes probably captured an aspect of classical economic thought in his statement of Say's Law, the classical economics embodied in Say's Law may well have been much more subtle than Keynes depicted it to be. (However the reader is referred to the earlier discussion of classical economics on pages 6 and 7 in which it was suggested that Keynes's main concern was to characterize the theoretical framework underlying classical economic thought, and not the whole of classical economics). Sowell does concede that 'the classical economists . . . probably assumed, separately from Say's Law, that full employment was normal or inevitable' (*ibid.*, p.210). Inasmuch as they believed this for reasons which were not concerned with the behaviour of the labour market, Keynes, in his statement of Say's Law, has probably captured an aspect of classical economic thought; whether this belief should be described as Say's Law or not is not a question which will concern us here.

There is a corollary to Say's Law, namely 'that any individual act of abstaining from consumption necessarily leads to, and amounts to the same thing as, causing the labour and commodities thus released from supplying consumption to be invested in the production of capital wealth' (G.T., p. 19). So an individual's decision to save more will lead to the community's becoming richer, since a corresponding amount of investment will be induced.

There are several arguments behind Say's Law and its corollary; Keynes discusses them and gives reasons for thinking that they do not work.

The major argument behind Say's Law has normally been held to be the one based on the fact that the major part of the demand for output comes from the factor incomes which are paid out in the process of production. If a manufacturer decides to increase output, he will pay out extra factor incomes sufficient to purchase the extra output. But this does not entail that if a manufacturer has excess capacity, or if there is unemployed labour, the manufacturer has an incentive to increase his output, for it is not necessarily true that if he expands his output, his extra revenue will cover his extra cost. It is of course true that 'the income derived in the aggregate by all the elements in the community concerned in a productive activity necessarily has a value exactly equal to the value of the output' (G.T., p. 20) — this is, indeed, the basic principle of national income accounting; however, this latter proposition in no way entails that manufacturers in such a position will actually have an incentive to increase output.

Keynes suggests that another reason for the plausibility of these doctrines is that 'these conclusions may have been applied to the kind of economy in which we actually live by false analogy from some kind of non-exchange Robinson Crusoe economy, in which the income which individuals consume or retain as a result of their productive activity is, actually and exclusively, the output *in specie* of that activity' (G.T., p. 20).

A reason for the plausibility of the corollary to Say's Law is that 'it is natural to suppose that the act of an individual, by which he enriches himself without apparently taking anything from anyone else, must also enrich the community as a whole' (G.T., pp. 20-1). But this again is fallacious: 'Those who think in this way ... are fallaciously supposing that there is a nexus which unites decisions to abstain from present consumption with decisions to provide for future consumption' (G.T., p. 21); we now know, being familiar with the ideas expressed in the General Theory, that an individual act of saving need not necessarily lead to an increase in aggregate saving; the initial act of saving may have a deflationary effect on the economy leading to lower saving elsewhere.

The corollary is really a consequence of Say's Law together with the normal national income identity. If income can be assumed to stay at its full employment level, an increase in savings must lead to an increase in investment.

So Keynes has basically three points to make against Say's Law and its corollary, or rather against the arguments which make these views seem plausible. The first is that the argument based on the circular flow of national income is insufficient to establish Say's Law; the second is that the conclusions may have been based on the illegitimate application of reasoning from a 'non-exchange Robinson Crusoe economy'; the third is that it is not necessarily true that an act of individual saving leads to an increase in the wealth of the community.

In the next chapter, chapter 3, Keynes proceeds to outline his framework for the analysis of the determination of the level of output and hence employment. In general, it allows the possibility of an under-employment equilibrium[1]. Say's Law can be stated within such a framework; it turns out to be true only under very restrictive conditions.

Keynes constructs the framework for his theory of output and employment by analysing the output and employment decisions of entrepreneurs. He does this by constructing aggregate demand and supply curves for output as a whole, the intersection of which will determine the level of output. He defines the aggregate supply price of a volume of output (corresponding to a certain level of employment) as 'the expectation of proceeds which will just make it worth the while of entrepreneurs to give that employment' (G.T., p. 24) and, where Z is the aggregate supply price of the output from employing N men, he describes the relationship between Z and N as the function $Z = \emptyset(N)$, the aggregate supply function. (The term 'aggregate supply price' may lead to confusion; it has the dimensions of price times quantity, and hence must be distinguished from the ordinary concept of supply price. This is what the first footnote of G.T., p. 24 warns against.)

An aggregate supply function can be constructed quite simply as follows: if we assume profit maximizing behaviour by entrepreneurs, they will employ labour until the real wage is equal to the marginal product of labour. So we have

$$w/p = F'(N) \tag{3.1}$$

Hence for employment to be N, the price of output must be $w/F'(N)$. So, for employers to offer an amount of employment N, they must expect to obtain total proceeds of an amount

$$Z = \frac{w}{F'(N)} F(N) \tag{3.2}$$

This, then, is the aggregate supply function.
  If, for example, $F(N) = AN^a$, $0 < a < 1$,

$$F'(N) = A_a N^{a-1} \tag{3.3}$$

and therefore we have the aggregate supply function

$$Z = \frac{w}{a} \cdot N \tag{3.4}$$

or, written in 'wage units', it is

$$Z_w = \frac{N}{a} \tag{3.5}$$

This is a linear aggregate supply function but, in general, of course, there is no reason why it should be linear.
  The aggregate demand function is defined as the relationship $D = f(N)$, where D are 'the proceeds entrepreneurs expect to receive from the employment of N men' (G.T., p. 25). This can be interpreted as the money value of the proceeds, so perhaps it should be written in the form $D = f(w, p, N)$; however, assuming that the real wage is equal to (or a function of) the marginal product of labour, we can write $p = g(w, N)$ and hence we can write the aggregate demand function in the form

$$D = f(w, N) \tag{3.6}$$

or in 'wage units',

$$D_w = \frac{f(w, M)}{w} \tag{3.7}$$

In this case, the value of aggregate demand may still depend on the level of the money wage, even though the aggregate demand function is written in wage units. This may be the case if, for example, there are real balance effects on consumption.

An aggregate demand curve has been drawn in Fig. 3.1. It will normally be an increasing function of N, with a slope of less than the money wage (that is, $f' < w$) in the Figure or less than unity in the case where the aggregate demand function is measured in 'wage units'. This ensures that, at least in the case depicted in the diagram, the aggregate demand and supply curves have a unique intersection. A justification for the assumption is provided by Keynes's 'fundamental psychological law', according to which the marginal propensity to consume is less than unity.

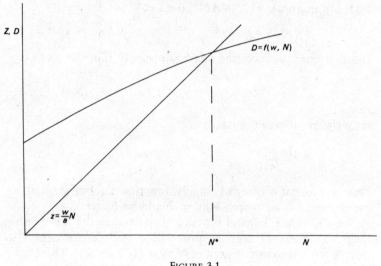

FIGURE 3.1

Keynes argues that there will be a tendency for entrepreneurs to expand production and employment if D is above Z; similarly if D is below Z, we would expect them to contract output and employment. Hence, provided that the equilibrium is a stable one, there will be a tendency for employment to settle at the point represented by the intersection of the two curves.

Keynes did not specify the precise dynamic mechanism whereby entrepreneurs were led to expand or contract output if aggregate demand and supply differed. Perhaps the following account provides a possible mechanism: entrepreneurs compute the total receipts to be derived from the output associated with a certain volume of employment. They do this successfully, if it is assumed that 'short term expectations are fulfilled'.[2] If expected receipts are greater than the aggregate supply price, then that means that the expected market price is greater than the (Marshallian) supply price, and hence entrepreneurs, with this expectation, are led to expand output. This process will continue until the point where the curves cross is reached.

This, then, is Keynes's theory of employment. Firms are assumed to maximize profits and in so doing produce at the point where the aggregate demand and supply curves intersect. The level of employment can then be determined via a production function. So in order to determine the volume of output and employment, we need to know what determines the level and shapes of the aggregate demand and supply curves. This is what much of the remainder of the General Theory is devoted to; this will be examined in later chapters.

It is perhaps important to note that the money-wage rate is an argument of both the aggregate supply function and the aggregate demand function as formulated here. This is not surprising, since it is the money value of receipts which is depicted on the vertical axis. This should not lead us to the conclusion, however, that an assumption of money wage rigidity underlies the analysis; to have a variable as an argument of a function is very different from assuming it to be constant. The framework will enable us to examine the effects of money-wage changes on output and employment, however, provided that we know how money-wage changes affect both the aggregate supply and the aggregate demand curves; hence Keynes's decision to leave his chapter on the effects of money-wage changes towards the end of the book, when the determinants of aggregate demand and supply had been analysed in more depth. We can therefore say that the theory is not predicated on an assumption of money-wage rigidity and that the theory can embody or incorporate a variety of assumptions about how the money-wage rate changes.

Say's Law can be stated within the aggregate demand and supply framework. It is, according to Keynes, that the aggregate demand and supply curves coincide, so 'competition between entrepreneurs would always lead to an expansion of employment up to the point at which the supply of output as a whole ceases to be elastic' (G.T., p. 26). We need not be concerned with whether this argument is correct; all we need to do is note that Say's Law requires very special conditions to hold if it is to be valid, and we have no reason at all for thinking that these conditions will, in fact, hold: 'If this is not the true law relating the aggregate demand and supply functions, there is a vitally important chapter of economic theory which remains to be written and without which all discussions concerning the volume of aggregate employment are futile' (G.T., p. 26).

There has been considerable debate in the literature on the nature of the Keynesian aggregate supply function; recent controversy has been inspired by Patinkin's treatment of the question; relevant references here are Patinkin (1976), pp.83-94, Roberts (1978), Patinkin (1978a) and Patinkin (1979). In his 1976 article, Patinkin rejected the interpretation of the aggregate supply curve along the lines given in this chapter, which has been based on entrepreneurs' maximizing behaviour, and instead interpreted it as the total variable cost curve.

A number of reasons can be given for doubting the account of the aggregate supply curve we have given in this chapter. First, 'the foregoing derivation attributes to Keynes an involved chain of mathematical reasoning which is entirely out of keeping with his usual analytical style' (Patinkin, 1979, p.159). Secondly, in defining aggregate supply price, Keynes defines it as 'the expectation of proceeds which will just make it worth the while of the entrepreneurs to give that employment' (G.T., p. 24) and it is not at all clear that this involves maximizing behaviour. Thirdly, when Keynes actually proceeds to specify the actual form of the aggregate supply function, (see G.T., p. 55 fn. 2) it is interpreted as the total variable cost curve. And fourthly, Keynes describes the point where the aggregate demand and supply curves cross at the point where 'the entrepreneurs' expectation of profit will be maximised' (G.T., p. 25). As Patinkin argues, this point may not in fact satisfy this condition. It is true that this point will generate higher profits than any lower point on the aggregate supply curve; however, if entrepreneurs produced a lower quantity, then receipts would be given not by the aggregate supply curve but by the aggregate demand curve, and it is quite possible that the profits thus generated will exceed profits at the intersection of the aggregate demand and aggregate supply curves. Of these reasons, the first two are not convincing. The mathematical reasoning involved in constructing the aggregate supply curve is not particularly involved or complicated and in putting it forward as an interpretation of what Keynes had in mind, one is not saying that he must have explicitly thought in these terms. One is rather putting it forward as a possible formalization of what he had in mind, in the sense that IS/LM may perhaps be regarded as a possible formalization of the Keynesian scheme. The phrase 'just make it worth the while' may be somewhat obscure; however, it does seem to be compatible with maximizing behaviour on the part of entrepreneurs. If entrepreneurs are considering which level of employment to offer, then in order to make it 'worth their while' to offer a particular level of employment rather than any other, that particular level of employment must be just more profitable than any other level of employment. Hence, it seems that such behaviour *is* compatible with maximizing behaviour. The third reason seems more weighty; it seems fairly clear 'that under the specified assumptions — which essentially imply that labour is the only variable factor of production the aggregate supply curve has a constant slope' (Patinkin, 1979, pp. 170-1) and this would seem to imply that the aggregate supply curve is coincident with the total variable cost curve. However, Roberts has given an interpretation of this footnote whereby it is argued to be compatible with the concept of an aggregate supply curve based on entrepreneurs' maximizing behaviour (see Roberts, 1978, p. 553). The fourth reason is perhaps more a reason for thinking that Keynes made a mistake when inserting the words 'the entrepreneurs' expectation of profits will be maximized' (G.T., p. 25). Patinkin gives reasons for thinking that these words should be deleted from the General Theory; perhaps these reasons are reasons for thinking that the words were added hastily, and therefore could quite likely involve a mistake. It was, perhaps, a very easy mistake to make; as has been argued already, a level of output characterized by the intersection of the AD and AS curves could be generated by entrepreneurs' profit maximizing behaviour and profits at this point are higher than profits represented by lower points on the AS curve. It is, moreover, difficult to see how Keynes could have made this mistake if the interpretation of the

AS curve as the total variable cost curve is adopted. There are other difficulties with the total variable cost curve interpretation of Keynes's AS curve. If Keynes did identify the AS curve with the total variable cost curve, it is difficult to make sense of the passage which states that if the AD and AS curves coincide, 'competition between entrepreneurs would always lead to an expansion of employment up to the point at which the supply of output as a whole ceases to be elastic' (G.T., p. 26); for under the total variable cost curve interpretation, every point on the AS curve is a point of zero profits, and there would seem to be no incentive to increase output. However, with the more normal interpretation of the AS curve, points on the AS curve associated with higher levels of output would be associated with higher profits, so entrepreneurs would have an incentive to increase output. (Although the actual dynamics behind the process are by no means clear.) Moreover, in no sense is the total variable cost curve a *supply* curve; it is very difficult, if not impossible, to think of any plausible theory of firms' behaviour which would lead them to behave in such a fashion.

So, while agreeing with Patinkin that Keynes's discussion of the AS curve is a confused one (see Patinkin, 1978a, p. 583), the conclusion which I would draw here is that the best interpretation is provided by the one which seeks to derive it, as has been done here, on the basis of profit-maximizing behaviour on the part of the entrepreneurs.

PART II

Say's Law is sometimes identified with what has come to be known as Walras' Law, which is a commonly accepted proposition of general equilibrium theory. This identification goes back at least as far as Clower (1965), and has been retained by a number of later writers (see, for example, Brothwell, 1975, p. 5). Walras' Law states that the market value of the sum of excess demands is zero, and can be written $p.z = 0$, where p is the vector of prices and z is the vector of excess demands. It can quite easily be derived from the premises that no agent is satisfied and that all profits are distributed (see, for example, Arrow and Hahn, 1971, pp. 20-1). But it must be emphasized — and this is a point which does not seem to have been recognized, at least in recent discussion — that Say's Law and Walras' Law are distinct. Say's Law is equivalent to the proposition that 'there is no such thing as involuntary unemployment in the strict sense' (G.T., p. 21) so that it is incompatible with excess supply in the labour market. Walras' Law is not incompatible with excess supply in the labour market; it is perfectly possible that $Zn < 0$, where n refers to the labour market; all it does entail is that if there is excess supply in the labour market, there must be excess demand in at least one other market. Hence Say's Law is incompatible with involuntary unemployment whereas Walras' Law is not. Hence we might say that Say's Law concerns the occurrence of non-clearing in the labour market, whereas Walras' Law concerns the implications of the non-clearing of various markets. There seems to be no evidence that Keynes was in fact aware of Walras' Law and the classical system he was attacking was certainly not Walras' general equilibrium system. The only reference to Walras in the General Theory is in a very different context (G.T., pp. 176-7). Hence, the problems which Clower considers arise in Keynesian economics through Keynes's apparent denial of a proposition which is 'a theorem which is susceptible of direct proof on the basis of premises which are typically taken as given in contemporary as well as classical price theory' (Clower, 1965, p. 278), do not arise. They do not arise because a similar claim has not been made for Say's Law and it is this which Keynes is attacking.

Keynes defines effective demand as 'the value of D at the point of the aggregate demand function, where it is intersected by the aggregate supply function' (G.T., p. 25). It is important to note that this notion of effective demand is different from Clower's. (This, again, is a point which does not seem to have been widely recognized.) Clower distinguishes between notional and effective excess demands; notional excess demand is the excess demand which would be exhibited by agents if they faced no quantity constraints on any market; their effective demands are those which they actually exhibit on the market. These may differ from their notional demands if agents face quantity constraints on at least one market. This distinction typically arises when a worker cannot sell all the labour he would like to sell at the existing prices; he therefore reduces his demand for consumption goods. His effective consumption function will have quantities as well as prices as arguments; we hence can derive a Keynesian-type consumption function. We may therefore say that in this case the consumption function exhibits the worker's effective demand for goods; this is different from the Keynesian concept of effective demand, which is that it is the sum of consumption and investment (and other components of aggregate demand) at the equilibrium level of output.

Keynes devotes a section of chapter 3 to discussing the classical economists' attitude to the concepts of aggregate and effective demand. It seems that they have largely ignored and neglected the concepts:

The idea that we can safely neglect the aggregate demand function is fundamental to the Ricardian economics, which underlie what we have been taught for more than a century.... The great puzzle of Effective Demand with which Malthus had wrestled vanished from economic literature. You will not find it mentioned even once in the whole works of Marshall, Edgeworth and Professor Pigou, from whose hands the classical theory has received its most mature embodiment. It could only live on furtively, below the surface, in the underworlds of Karl Marx, Silvio Gesell or Major Douglas. (G.T., p.32).

The interpretation propounded here can help explain the classical economists' neglect of the problem of effective demand. The concepts of aggregate demand and supply curves are used to determine the equilibrium level of income when there is involuntary unemployment. If we can be assured of the maintenance of the full employment level of income, then the concepts become redundant; the level of employment is already determined. Hence the classical economists with a theoretical apparatus based on an assumption of full employment, had no use for the concept. However, economists not so closely linked to the classical school, who did not use a theoretical apparatus based on this assumption had an inkling that there was something in the concept; they therefore applied it but perhaps were not aware of the full theoretical significance of the concept.

So in chapter 3 Keynes introduces the concepts of aggregate demand and supply in a theoretically rigorous fashion; this is a theory of the determination of the level of income and employment when the labour market may not clear. They were only introduced after he had argued for the relaxation of the labour market clearing assumption. It follows, then, that it is incorrect to use the concepts of aggregate demand and supply in discussing

Keynes's objections to the classical theory of employment. This is what Hansen seems to do when he writes: 'If the utility of the current real wage is exactly equal to the marginal disutility of labour, it would not be possible to increase employment by raising Aggregate Demand' (Hansen, 1953, p. 22), and 'The manipulation of wage rates is, therefore, he thought, not an effective way to increase employment. Manipulation of Demand is a far more effective policy' (*ibid.*, p. 23).

However, Keynes's criticism of the classical theory of employment precedes his development of the aggregate demand/supply framework; hence we can discount Hansen's interpretation of Keynes's arguments for rejecting the classical theory of employment. His remarks may constitute a correct statement of the conclusion Keynes reaches in chapter 19; however, these are conclusions he reaches through his aggregate demand and supply framework; they are not relevant to his discussion of the classical theory of the labour market; it was because he found the classical theory inadequate that he developed his theory of output and employment; his theory therefore cannot be presumed in expounding his criticism of the classical theory of employment.

Perhaps, finally, we might comment on Patinkin's remark that: 'despite Keynes' declared objective of integrating monetary and value theory, he did not really develop a theory of the demand for labour consistent with the state of unemployment qua market disequilibrium that was his major concern in the General Theory' (Patinkin, 1976, p. 94). Patinkin's argument for this conclusion seems to be that if Keynes were to be consistent in his attempt to construct a theory of the workings of an economy in disequilibrium, he should have modified his theory of the demand for labour in order to take account of the possibility that firms might not be able to sell the output they would like to sell at the market price. However, Keynes's concern was to analyse the working of an economy in which just the labour market fails to clear; he retained the assumption that other markets clear and hence the assumption that the real wage is equal to the marginal product of labour is entirely appropriate.

So, to sum up on Say's Law and aggregate demand and supply curves: Say's Law states that the economy will tend automatically to a full employment level of output; Keynes argues, not so much that it is necessarily false, but that we have no reason for thinking that it is true. He establishes a framework for determining the level of output and employment and argues that Say's Law would mean that the underlying curves would have very special shapes which we have no *a priori* reason to suppose that they should have.

The structure and purpose of the rest of the General Theory now become clearer. In order to determine the level of output and employment, it is necessary to discuss the determinants of the shapes and levels of the aggregate demand and supply curves. Chapters 8 to 10 look at the behaviour of one component of aggregate demand, consumption, whereas chapters 11 and 12 examine the determinants of the other main component, investment. The interest rate is of obvious relevance for the level of investment, hence chapters 13 to 15 are devoted to the determination of the interest rate. Chapters of a slightly more speculative nature follow (chapters 16 and 17), and there is a summary of the General Theory in chapter 18. Only in chapter 19 is the effect of money-wage changes on output and employment considered. The aggregate supply function and its inverse, the employment function are discussed in chapter 20, and the theory of prices is developed in chapter 21. Some 'Short Notes suggested by the General Theory' conclude the book.

In the next chapter, Keynes's analysis of the components of aggregate demand will be discussed at greater length.

NOTES

1 Readers are referred back to our earlier discussion of the concept of equilibrium on pp. 12-13. If by equilibrium we mean a situation where all the equations which characterize a model are mutually satisfied, then in the absence of a labour clearing condition, there is no reason why an equilibrium should not involve involuntary unemployment.

2 There has been some controversy over whether Keynes actually made this assumption (on this, see Patinkin, 1976, p. 140; Roberts, 1978, pp. 569-70). Roberts seems to be correct in arguing that Keynes, in his 1937 lecture notes does not state that he assumed that short-term expectations are always fulfilled when writing the General Theory but rather that 'the theory of effective demand is substantially the same if we assume that short period expectations are always fulfilled'.

4 The Components of Aggregate Demand

In this chapter, Keynes's analysis of the components of aggregate demand, consumption and investment, will be discussed; this analysis is contained mainly in chapters 8 to 12 of the General Theory. Although Keynes's Book IV, which is called 'The inducement to Invest', extends until chapter 18, only chapters 11 and 12 are concerned with the investment function itself; the later chapters deal mainly with money and the interest rate, topics which will be considered in the next chapter of this book. First, an exposition of Keynes's treatment of the consumption function and the associated multiplier will be given. Then, some of the literature on this topic will be discussed. Keynes's discussion of investment will be treated similarly, though here the discussion will be briefer, since the topic presents fewer problems from an exegetical point of view.

PART I

Keynes commences his first chapter on consumption by summarizing his conclusion so far 'that the volume of employment is determined by the point of intersection of the aggregate supply function with the aggregate demand function' (G.T., p. 89). Since 'the aggregate supply function ... involves few considerations which are not already familiar' (*ibid.*) the bulk of the remainder of the book is devoted to analysing the components of the aggregate demand function. Since this relates aggregate demand to employment, it would seem that the consumption function would relate consumption and employment. However, Keynes decides that it will be more convenient to relate consumption and income. This is legitimate if income is a monotonic function of employment; Keynes considers the possibility that income might not even be a function of employment alone — 'two different distributions of a given aggregate employment N between different employment might ... lead to different values of Y' (G.T., p. 90) — but considers it a good approximation to regard income as uniquely determined by N. So he postulates a consumption function of the form:

$$C = f(Y)$$

where C and Y are measured in 'wage units'. Note that it is assumed that the function has this form; an argument is not presented for such a relationship (apart from the argument relating Y and N). It follows from the way the aggregate demand function is defined with aggregate demand dependent upon employment; but even there the dependence is assumed and not argued for.

So, having postulated such a consumption function, he proceeds to discuss the factors which influence the shape and form of this function. He distinguishes between 'objective' and 'subjective' factors; the distinction between these can perhaps be illustrated in the following way (this is the author's own way of interpreting Keynes's distinction). Supposing we were to attempt to construct a fully specified consumption function:

$$C = f(Y, \ldots),$$

then the objective factors would be those which we would tend to enter as arguments into the function — we might include the rate of interest, wealth, the rate of inflation etc. — whereas the subjective factors, which Keynes describes as 'those psychological characteristics of human nature and those special practices and institutions which, though not unalterable, are unlikely to undergo a material change over a short period of time except in abnormal or revolutionary circumstances' (G.T., p. 91), will still affect the functional form itself.

Keynes lists and discusses a number of objective factors which might be expected to affect the propensity to consume. He considers factors such as 'windfall changes in capital values' and substantial changes in the rate of interest and in fiscal policy, but his conclusion is that although such factors may make some difference, 'the amount of aggregate consumption mainly depends on the amount of aggregate income, changes in the propensity itself being treated as a secondary influence' (G.T., p. 96). This is a conclusion he reiterates in his *Quarterly Journal of Economics* article of 1937: 'People's propensity to spend is influenced by many factors such as the distribution of income, their normal attitude to the future and — although probably in a minor degree — by the rate of interest. But in the main, the prevailing psychological law seems to be that when aggregate income increases, consumption expenditure will also increase' (Keynes, 1937, p. 222). So Keynes emphasizes income as the major factor influencing consumption; his consideration of other factors stems perhaps more from a desire to be comprehensive than from a belief that they are of importance[1].

Having assumed that it is income which is the major influence on consumption, Keynes then discusses the exact form of the function. He introduces his 'fundamental psychological law', which is that the marginal propensity to consume is between zero and one; it is that which is crucial for his theory. He goes on to make further conjectures about the shape of the function and suggests that the average propensity to consume will decrease with income. He later suggests that the marginal propensity to consume may also decline with income (G.T., p. 120). But as he emphasizes in a letter which appears in his Collected Works (see Moggridge, 1973, p. 275), these conjectures are in no way essential to his theory; what is crucial is the 'fundamental psychological law' which will become a stability condition for the Keynesian system.

The next step in the construction of the theory is the introduction of the concept of the multiplier. Keynes has already established that if employment is to increase, a rise in consumption must be accompanied by a rise in investment. The multiplier shows us by how much income will increase for a given increase in investment. It is hence a purely logical consequence of the theoretical system Keynes has set up. Suppose we have a consumption function of the form

$$C = a + bY \qquad (4.1)$$

and the following is the national income equilibrium condition

$$C+I=Y \qquad (4.2)$$

This is basically equation (1.5) of the classical system from chapter 1, with the dependence of C and I on the interest rate suppressed. In the Keynesian system this becomes the condition that aggregate demand is equal to aggregate supply.

Then, as a matter of logic, it follows that

$$Y=\frac{a+I}{1-b} \qquad (4.3)$$

and $1/(1-b)$ may be defined as the multiplier. It shows how much equilibrium national income increases for a given increase in a component of autonomous expenditure; it does not contain any new information about the system under consideration; instead, it is a neat way of summarizing information about the system; in this respect the concept of the multiplier is somewhat like that of elasticity.

Although the consumption function may be said to have originated with Keynes, the same cannot be said of the concept of the multiplier; the concept had already been introduced by Kahn in 1931 (see Kahn, 1931), but in this case it related the total increase in employment to the increase in one specific part of the labour force, that in the investment industries. Keynes describes this as the employment multiplier, in contrast to his own investment multiplier, and argues that there is no reason to suppose that the two have the same value; nevertheless, in his analysis he deals with the simplified case where they do have the same value.

The fact that the concept of the multiplier was already in existence when the General Theory was written and the fact that the multiplier follows logically from the examination of a theoretical system which was only introduced in that book are not incompatible. It is fairly intuitive that if there is an increase in employment in one sector of the economy, there may result a general increase in employment as the newly employed increase their consumption demands; fairly intuitive, that is, for those not accustomed to using a theoretical apparatus, as the classical economists did, based on the (perhaps tacit) assumption of full employment. If there is a fairly stable relationship between the two then one can call the ratio the multiplier; however, it is a further step to construct a theoretical schema which generates such a result; and Keynes may take the credit for having done this. This is basically in accord with Patinkin's analysis of the genesis of the multiplier concept (see Patinkin, 1977; Patinkin, 1978b). Patinkin argues against the view that Kahn's 1931 article represented recognition of the theory of effective demand. He contends that the basic idea of the multiplier was already in circulation before 1931 and that Kahn's main achievement was in showing it to be greater than unity but finite. Kahn presented what might be described as the dynamic multiplier — the sum of an infinite series — and not the comparative statics multiplier, which is what has been presented here.

Keynes elaborates on the concept of the multiplier and examines the workings of his (as yet) simple theory of income determination, that contained basically in equations (4.1) and (4.2). It nevertheless enables conclusions fundamentally different from those of the classical theory to be reached; consider, for example, his discussion of the employment creating effects of public works in the last section of chapter 10. Keynes writes later: 'the psychological law was of the utmost importance in the development of my own thought' (Keynes, 1937a, p. 222) and it is perhaps possible to see why; with the consumption function it was possible to construct a theory of output and employment which differed radically from received doctrine, yet which seemed consistent with experience and enabled concepts which were already in circulation, like the multiplier, to be rigorously derived. This was before the theory of liquidity preference, for example, had been developed: 'The initial novelty lies in my maintaining that it is ... the level of incomes which ensures equality between savings and investment. The arguments which lead up to this initial conclusion are independent of my subsequent theory of the rate of interest, and in fact I reached if before I had reached the latter theory' (Keynes, 1937b, p. 250). It must nevertheless have convinced Keynes that he was on to something of importance and that if he persisted he could construct a complete theory of employment, interest and money.

Keynes emphasizes that a distinction ought to be drawn between the logical theory of the multiplier and the actual course of events whereby an increase in investment leads to the full multiplier increase in national income. The time path of the increase will depend, at least partly, on whether the increase is foreseen or not. He considers the case where the increase in investment and the consequent rise in demand for goods is entirely unforeseen so that there is no initial increase in the production of consumer goods (G.T., pp. 122-5). The attempt of those newly employed in the capital goods industry to consume more than they otherwise would will presumably raise the prices of consumer goods. This may lead to a postponement or reduction of consumption and also to a partial destocking in the consumer goods industries. Hence, the increase in investment does not initially lead to the full multiplier increase in national income; there is a partially offsetting decline in stocks and a fall in the multiplier, due to a (temporary) fall in the marginal propensity to consume. The full increase in national income only comes through in the long run when the consumer goods industry has also expanded. So there is a multiplier equation which always holds, regardless of the time-period considered; the predictive power of a theory such as that represented by equations (4.1) and (4.2), where I represents investment in the capital goods industries and b represents the 'normal' marginal propensity to consume, is confined to the longer run. We may note here, somewhat parenthetically, that Keynes does not consider the possibility that the goods market may not clear and that, for example, firms may desire to supply more goods at the market price than consumers wish to demand. There are several reasons for thinking that Keynes assumed the commodity market to clear continuously. First, in passages like this when Keynes could have considered the possibility that the market might not clear, he did not do so. Secondly, he used the condition that the marginal product of labour is equal to the real wage which precludes excess supply or demand in the goods market. Thirdly, he gave reasons, discussed in our chapter 2, for constructing a model of the workings of an economy in which the labour market might not clear; no such reasons have been given for considering an economy in which the goods market does not clear as well.

PART II

There are two main problems in Keynesian exegesis concerning the consumption function. First, it seems fairly obvious that consumption should be a function of income, so obvious that the consumption function was almost immediately adopted as a key economic relationship; why then was it only Keynes, and not some previous economist, who was the first to postulate such a relationship? Secondly, there is the problem of assessing the importance of the consumption function in Keynesian economics. These questions (and some of the related literature) will be discussed in turn.

Keynes himself believed that the consumption function was an obvious construction — he refers to 'this extremely obvious postulate' (Keynes, 1937a, p. 222) — and it is noteworthy that he nowhere argues for a dependence of consumption on income. He assumes such a relationship, and although it might be argued that the relationship follows directly from his postulation of an aggregate demand function with employment as its argument, investment is also a component of aggregate demand, but this is not considered to be a function of the level of employment when Keynes analyses it in chapters 11 and 12.

Klein provides one reason for the obviousness of the consumption function:

From the accepted theories of consumer behaviour it is learned that if a household maximises its satisfaction (or preferences) subject to the constraint that its budget does not exceed its income, then the demand for each type of good consumed by a particular household will depend upon the household income and the prices of all goods in the household budget (Klein, 1966, p. 58).

But if this is the rationale behind the consumption function, it is very hard to see why the classical economists did not also postulate such a consumption function, for in the quotation above, a standard theory of consumer behaviour with which the classical economists would surely have been familiar, is being applied.

The explanation which will be propounded here is that the consumption function may appear obvious when the type of problem Keynes was concerned with, that of examining the behaviour of an economy in which the labour market may not clear, is considered, but does not appear so obvious when an economy in which all markets clear is considered. The argument will depend heavily on Clower (1965).

In general equilibrium, when all markets clear, agents' demand functions for consumption goods will have relative prices and initial endowments as their arguments. The actual quantities of factors sold will not be relevant. However, suppose we allow for the possibility of trading at 'false' prices when some markets do not clear. Specifically, let us assume that an agent cannot sell as much of a factor as he would like to at the market price; he is constrained in his supply of the factor. This will be an additional constraint the agent will face in his maximizing behaviour; the quantity of the factor which he can sell will hence be an argument of his consumption function.

A neoclassical consumption function might be written as

$$C = f(P_1, \ldots, P_n; e) \qquad (4.4)$$

which states that the demand for consumption goods is a function of the current and expected future prices of the consumption good and labour and also of the endowments (e).

Suppose now a household experiences a constraint on the amount of labour it can sell in the present ($\bar{n}$) but does not expect any such constraints to prevail in the future. Then its consumption function might be written

$$C = g(P_1, \ldots, P_n; e; \bar{n}) \qquad (4.5)$$

and by changing the functional form slightly, (4.5) can be written in the form

$$C = g'(P_1, \ldots, P_n; e; P_n \bar{n}) \qquad (4.5')$$

where P_n is the current (money-)wage.

So we have a consumption function with the earnings of labour explicitly incorporated into the function; this may be identified with income if we assume that the endowments do not generate incomes.

In the general equilibrium case, labour supply will be a choice variable, so we can write

$$n = n(P_1, \ldots, P_n; e) \qquad (4.6)$$

and if we define income, y, by

$$\gamma = P_n n(P_1, \ldots, P_n; e) \qquad (4.7)$$

it may be possible to write

$$P_1 = j(P_2, \ldots, P_n; e; \gamma) \qquad (4.8)$$

and hence incorporating this into the general equilibrium consumption function, we might obtain

$$C = f(j(P_2, \ldots, P_n; e; \gamma), P_2, \ldots, P_n; e; \gamma)$$
$$\equiv f'(P_2, \ldots, P_n; e; \gamma) \qquad (4.4')$$

so here we have a neoclassical consumption function with income as an independent argument. The difference between the Keynesian and the neoclassical consumption function is sometimes expressed by the statement that in the Keynesian case, income is an independent argument; this is evidently based on a comparison of functions of the form of equations (4.4) and (4.5'). However, we have derived a neoclassical consumption function (see equation (4.4')), which has income as an independent argument. But this is only so because we have eliminated P_1. The difference might perhaps better be expressed as follows: provided that we are comparing consumption functions which contain as their arguments all prices faced by agents and endowments, then the Keynesian one will also contain income as an independent argument; in the neoclassical case, income will be a function of prices and endowments and hence will not be an independent argument of the consumption function.

So, we might argue, it is only in a non-market clearing context that one would be likely to think of consumption as a function of income; as Keynes was the first to explore systematically the workings of an economy in which one market could fail to clear, it is entirely comprehensible that he should come up with such a consumption function. (We are not saying that Keynes thought explicitly in these terms, rather that Clower's analysis makes it plausible that he should have constructed the type of theory he did). Hence we may concur with Clower's statement that Keynes had a dual decision theory at the back of his mind when he wrote the General Theory (Clower, 1965, p. 290). (The dual decision theory is the theory that when people find that they cannot fulfil their general equilibrium demands, because of non-market clearing, they recompute them, taking the additional constraints they perceive into account; hence the dual decision hypothesis is basically the view we have expressed above.)

But it is important to note that the dual decision hypothesis has been argued to be important just as an underpinning of the consumption function. Clower writes:

It is another question whether Keynes can reasonably be considered to have had a dual decision theory of household behaviour at the back of his mind when he wrote the 'General Theory'. For my part, I do not think there can be any doubt that he did, although I can find no direct evidence in any of his writings to show that he ever thought explicitly in these terms. But indirect evidence is available in almost unlimited quantity: in his discussion of 'Say's Law', his development of the consumption function concept, his account of interest theory and his discussion of wage and price determination (Clower, 1965, p. 290).

We have agreed with Clower that the dual decision hypothesis provides a rigorous underpinning for the consumption function, and that Keynes can be interpreted as having, at least implicitly, thought in those terms. But no argument has been presented to show that the dual decision hypothesis is relevant for the analysis of any component of Keynes's theory apart from that of consumption.

There does seem to be some uncertainty in the literature, however, on what has or has not been established by Clower and on the precise relevance of the dual decision hypothesis. Two questions in particular which ought to be tackled are those of the relationship between the dual decision hypothesis and the perfection of capital markets and the relevance of the economy's being a monetary one.

First, despite assertions to the contrary, the dual decision hypothesis is not predicated on an assumption of imperfect capital markets. Current income can still be expected to have an effect on consumption even if capital markets are perfect. If a household experiences a constraint on the amount of labour it can sell, then the amount of wealth which the household can spend over its lifetime on consumption will fall and hence we would expect it to revise its inter-temporal consumption pattern. However, the degree of perfection or imperfection of capital markets may certainly affect the form of the consumption function (see, for example, Flemming, 1973). A second point is that with perfect capital markets, a constraint on current labour supply may be a reason for consuming *more*, not less, in the current period. (I am indebted to John Flemming for this point.) This may arise if leisure and consumption are complementary; extra enforced leisure will require extra consumption, and with perfect capital markets this can be financed.

Sometimes it seems to be asserted that the dual decision hypothesis has something intrinsically to do with the economy's being a monetary one. This, again, is a mistake; the dual decision hypothesis has nothing to do with the economy's being monetary or not. It basically concerns an implication of a market's not clearing; a worker who becomes increasingly constrained in his labour supply might be expected to change his consumption behaviour in a barter economy as well as in a monetary economy. The idea that the dual decision hypothesis may have something to do with the economy's being a monetary one may have risen through being confused with Clower's dictum 'Money buys goods and goods buy money; but goods do not buy goods' (Clower, 1967, pp. 207-8). However, this aphorism appears in a different article; it has nothing to do with the dual decision hypothesis.

The area seems to be one in which confusion continues to pervade the literature. Consider the following description of Clower's arguments:

(1) All neo-Walrasian models have structurally similar feasible choice sets defined by the appropriate budget constraints.
(2) In neo-Walrasian analysis, since no trades are carried on except at equilibrium prices, the constraint on household purchases is *realised* income.
(3) Since prices only 'existed' in equilibrium, Walras' Law always holds.
(4) Consequently, unemployment is impossible unless there are market rigidities or failures.
(5) Thus, 'either Walras' Law is incompatible with Keynesian economics, or Keynes had nothing fundamentally new to add to orthodox economic theory' (Weintraub, 1979, p. 76).

As the argument stands — I am not concerned with the question of how accurately Clower's argument has been reproduced — there are several serious mistakes.

First, it is not true that 'the constraint on household purchases is realised income' in any type of model discussed by Clower. Households are always constrained by a budget constraint; in the case where they cannot sell all the labour they desire at the going price (this pre-supposes trading at disequilibrium prices), realised income will be an *independent argument* of the consumption function, not a constraint on consumption.

Secondly, the validity of Walras' Law has nothing to do with prices 'existing' in equilibrium (whatever that may mean). As already argued, it can be proved quite simply on the basis of the assumptions that households exhaust their budget constraints and that all profits are distributed, and it will hold both in and out of equilibrium.

Thirdly, Walras' Law says nothing about the conditions under which unemployment is possible. It implies that if there is unemployment, then this implies that there must be excess demand (of some sort!) elsewhere in the economy. Walras' Law is relevant in considering the implications of disequilibrium in the labour market; it does not have anything to say on the conditions under which disequilibrium is likely to arise. Hence point 4 does not follow from point 3.

Fourthly, as has already been argued, Clower erred in identifying Say's Law and Walras' Law; hence Clower's 'post-Keynesian dilemma' does not arise.

I now turn to consider some of the literature which has discussed Clower's contribution and the dual decision hypothesis.

Grossman has argued against the view that Keynes had a dual decision hypothesis 'at the back of his mind' when writing the General Theory. He argues that Keynes's formulation of the consumption function was simply ad hoc, and he had nothing like the dual decision hypothesis in mind when writing the General Theory (Grossman, 1972, p. 29). His reason seems to be that if this were indeed Keynes's line of thought, he would have generalized it and applied it to the analysis of firms' demand for labour as well, in the way Patinkin did, in Patinkin (1965), where firms may be constrained in the amount of output they can sell at the going price and a fall in demand may therefore lead to a decline in output and employment with no change in prices. However, this ignores the fact that Keynes gave specific reasons for analysing an economy in which the labour market might not clear (compare our analysis in chapter 2). However, he did, as we have seen, retain the assumption that other markets cleared; there is no non-price rationing of commodity demand. So the reason Keynes applied the dual decision hypothesis only in the case of the labour market was that he saw his task as the analysis of an economy with just the labour market not clearing. He set up the theory to analyse the determination of the level of unemployment and he assumed that other markets cleared. It is hence comprehensible that he should, if only implicitly, apply the Clower device, which is relevant when it is the labour market which does not clear, and not the Patinkin device which relates to the case of the commodity market's non-clearing. Hence we must reject Grossman's argument that Keynes's formulation of the consumption function was simply ad hoc.

The second question is that of assessing the importance of the consumption function in and for Keynesian economics.

Keynes considered the consumption function to be of fundamental importance: 'This psychological law was of the utmost importance in the development of my own thought, and it is, I think, absolutely fundamental to the theory of effective demand as set forth in my book' (Keynes, 1937a, p. 222). Brothwell concurs with this point of view: 'Keynes' consumption function is fundamental to the theory of effective demand' (Brothwell, 1975); however, there are dissenters: Minsky writes: '. . . in no sense is the consumption function "the heart of modern macroeconomics"' (Minsky, 1975, p. 23). He considers that Keynes's treatment of investment was more important than his treatment of consumption. His reason seems to be that the Book on investment is much longer than the Book on consumption (see Minsky, 1975, p. 25). But this is a spurious reason, even if we accept the extremely dubious premiss that the amount of space an author devotes to a topic is a good indicator of the relative importance he accords to that topic. It is true that Book III is only forty-two pages long, whereas Book IV is 119 pages long, but only the first two chapters of Book IV deal explicitly with investment; the remaining chapters are devoted to money and interest and there is a concluding chapter summarizing the General Theory; in fact the first two chapters cover only twenty-nine pages, so in fact Keynes devotes less space to investment than to consumption. An argument produced by Bliss is perhaps more important (see Bliss, 1975, pp. 207-8); this is construed as an argument against Clower's view that the dual decision hypothesis is the essence of Keynesian economics but can also be construed as an argument against the view that the consumption function is of crucial importance in Keynesian economics.

Bliss constructs a Rent-a-Man economy in which the dual decision hypothesis is negated; in this economy, people are paid whether they are employed or not; hence a fall in employment will not produce a decline in disposable income and therefore there will be no decline in consumption. This is equivalent to the aggregate demand schedule being horizontal, as illustrated in Fig. 4.1. Of course, there is no reason why involuntary unemployment should not occur in such an economy; it is perfectly possible that aggregate demand could be insufficient to generate full employment, as illustrated in the diagram.

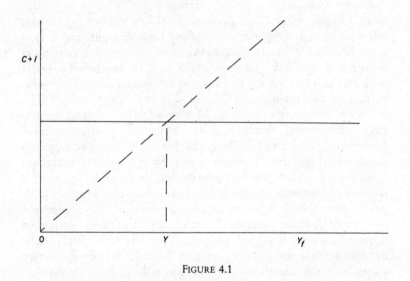

FIGURE 4.1

So the argument is successful in showing that it is not the dual decision hypothesis and the associated consumption function which account for the difference between Keynes and the classics; even in the absence of a process of the type described by Clower involuntary unemployment would still be possible. However, although it is not the consumption function which is Keynes's crucial point of divergence from the classics, this does not mean that the consumption function is not important in the system Keynes set up to determine the level of output and employment. It is rather difficult to answer the question as to which is the most important equation in the set of simultaneous equations constituting a model; they are all important, and the equilibrium values of the variables will normally change whenever one of the constituent equations is changed. If one is comparing two sets of equations, one might focus attention on those equations which differ; and if one is comparing the Keynesian and the classical systems, one might therefore pick out the consumption function, since in the Keynesian system, the role of income and its effect on consumption are emphasized. However, the consumption function is not the only modification made in the Keynesian system, and as Bliss's argument shows, it is insufficient, on its own, to account for the difference between Keynes and the classics. The interpretation presented here is that major emphasis should be placed on Keynes's relaxation of the labour-market clearing assumption, and that the other points of divergence between Keynes's system and the classical system can in some way be attributed to this. This is perfectly consistent with Bliss's argument. This is not to deny Keynes's statement of the importance of the consumption function in the development of his own thought; with the development of this concept, he had enough material for the construction of a simple model which generated results significantly different from those of the classical school; although at that stage much of the theoretical structure of the General Theory was yet to be constructed, it at least gave him the feeling that if he persisted he could construct an adequate theory of employment which would contrast markedly with that produced by the classical economists.

Nevertheless, the idea has been expressed that the fact that in Keynesian analysis quantities, as well as prices, enter as arguments in the consumption function, constitutes the crucial difference between Keynesian and Classical economics. For example, Clower writes: 'an essential formal difference between Keynesian and orthodox economics is that market excess demands are in general assumed to depend on current market transactions in the former, to be independent of current market transactions in the latter' (Clower, 1965, p. 294). Leijonhufvud makes basically the same point: 'the fundamental distinction between general equilibrium and Keynesian models ... lies in the appearance of quantity variables in the excess demand relations of the latter' (Leijonhufvud, 1968, p. 51).

This calls for two observations. First, quantity variables do not appear in all Keynesian excess demand functions; there is no reason for thinking, for example, that quantities should appear in the excess demand for labour function. Secondly, according to the interpretation presented in this book, the fundamental difference between Keynesian and classical models is that in the latter case, all markets clear, whereas in the Keynesian case, the labour market may fail to clear; it is a consequence of this fundamental difference that the excess demand functions for consumption goods should differ between the two cases; so inasmuch as the above statements by Clower and Leijonhufvud are correct, they are compatible with the interpretation propounded here.

PART III

The next topic to be discussed is Keynes's analysis of investment. His discussion of investment might be considered to be an advance on the classical treatment of the subject, but he does not consider that his treatment of investment represents an important divergence from the classical theory; he is basically developing a theory the essentials of which were already in existence.

Investment, according to Keynes, depends on the prospective yields of capital assets on the one hand, and on the supply prices of the capital assets on the other. He defines the marginal efficiency of capital as 'that rate of discount which would make the present value of the series of annuities given by the returns expected from the capital-asset during its life just equal to its supply price' (G.T., p. 135). Investment will take place until the MEC is brought into equality with the rate of interest; it will normally decline as investment increases for two reasons. First, as the quantity of capital increases, the yield will fall, and secondly, as more capital goods are produced, the supply price of capital will rise, 'the second of these factors being usually the more important in the short run, but the longer the period in view the more does the first factor take its place' (G.T., p. 136). This calls for two comments. Later discussions of investment have distinguished between the marginal efficiency of capital and the marginal efficiency of investment. See, for example, Shapiro (1978), pp. 165-74. The appropriate criterion then becomes that the marginal efficiency of investment should be equated to the interest rate. Keynes's discussion of what he calls the marginal efficiency of capital shows that what he had in mind was what is now known as the marginal efficiency of investment and hence his use of the term 'marginal efficiency of capital' is not incorrect, although perhaps confusing. The second point to note is Keynes's stress on supply side factors in producing equality between the MEC and the interest rate in the short run. This calls into question Leijonhufvud's claim that capital assets and bonds are highly substitutable in the General Theory, so much so that they can be aggregated (see Leijonhufvud, 1968, pp. 111-85), for if asset-holders regard two assets as highly substitutable, then it will be impossible for the price of one to rise significantly relative to that of the other for supply side reasons as long as both assets continue to be held.

Keynes does not seem to think that his treatment of investment in any way represents an important divergence from the classical school and relates his discussion to that of other writers; he believes the account he has given is fairly similar to that given by both Irving Fisher and Marshall, although 'there is ... a remarkable lack of any clear account of the matter' (G.T., p. 139) — however, Alchian argues that Keynes has misinterpreted Fisher (see Alchian, 1955). So Keynes, in his chapters on investment, regards himself not so much as constructing a new theory of investment, but in clarifying and developing a theory the essentials of which were contained in previous work and could equally well have supported the classical theory's view of investment which, as we have seen, related investment to the interest rate. This is entirely comprehensible, given the nature of the task Keynes had set himself; non-clearing in the labour market has certain implications as far as consumption is concerned, and hence Keynes introduced his consumption function, which was an innovation, but does not lead to any such modifications for the theory of investment.

Two further points to consider in Keynes's treatment of investment are his treatment of expectations and the relevance of the distinction which is sometimes made between the real and the nominal interest rate.

Taking the latter topic first, Keynes does mention Fisher's distinction between the money and the real interest rate, but argues that 'it is difficult to make sense of this theory as stated, because it is not clear whether the change in the value of money is or is not assumed to be foreseen' (G.T., p. 142). The distinction between the money and the real interest rate is not a theory, though; it is definitional; the real interest rate is defined to be the money interest rate adjusted for inflation. What Keynes is perhaps objecting to is the theory that the money interest rate will adjust fully to the rate of inflation, so that the real interest rate is invariant with respect to the rate of inflation. His argument is that if the prospective change in the value of money is not foreseen, it will have no effect on current affairs, whereas if it is foreseen:

the prices of existing goods will be forthwith so adjusted that the advantages of holding money and of holding goods are again equalised, and it will be too late for holders of money to gain or to suffer a change in the rate of interest which will offset the prospective change during the period of the loan in the value of the money lent (G.T., p.142).

This is an interesting argument against the Fisher view that the real interest rate is invariant with respect to (fully anticipated) inflation, and it would seem to be, at least on certain premisses, correct. If it suddenly becomes expected that goods prices will rise at a steady rate, then one would expect people to try to switch out of money into goods; however, with fixed supplies of these, at least in the short run, the relative attractiveness of holding each must remain constant, which implies a zero rate of increase of goods' prices; hence goods' prices must rise instantly by the full amount of the expected change in prices. However, it is possible to think of various qualifications to this argument; if people are interested in their real money balances, then with a higher level of goods' prices, people will want to hold a higher nominal quantity of money. With a constant nominal stock of money, equilibrium requires that the holding of money becomes more costly, which may entail *some* inflation of goods' prices. If this is so, bond holding will become relatively less attractive; hence one would expect bond prices to fall and the interest rate to rise. Hence, by relaxing one of the assumptions underlying Keynes's argument, one can generate some degree of correlation between expected inflation and the interest rate. The inflationary experience of the post-war era has perhaps convinced most economists that there is this correlation between expected inflation and the nominal interest rate, but that the effect of a rise in expected inflation on the interest rate is likely to be less than proportional. An argument, similar to Keynes's, based on the existence of an asset with a fixed nominal return, could perhaps explain this observation.

So Keynes does not seem to acknowledge an effect of inflation on the nominal rate of interest. Keynes suggests instead that inflation will affect investment through its effect on the marginal efficiency of capital. If inflation raises the marginal efficiency of capital and does not induce a similar rise in the rate of interest, investment will rise. But whether inflation *does* raise the marginal efficiency of capital depends very much on how it is defined. If the returns which are discounted back to the present in computing the marginal efficiency of capital are measured in terms of the prices which are then expected to prevail, then it is true that inflation will normally increase the marginal efficiency of capital. If, however, the returns are measured in terms of current prices, then the MEC should not change with the rate of inflation. But in this latter case, the appropriate investment criterion is that the MEC should be equated to the *real* rate of interest, and given Keynes's argument that the nominal rate of interest will be unaffected by inflation, it follows that Keynes would expect inflation to depress the real rate of interest. So Keynes's way of analysing the effect of inflation on investment and that where the MEC, appropriately defined, is compared with the real rate of interest, amount essentially to the same thing. This point will be relevant when we come to consider the effect of deflation on investment and aggregate demand.

Keynes devotes a chapter to expectations and their effect on investment. He emphasizes 'the extreme precariousness of the basis of knowledge on which our estimates of prospective yield have to be made' (G.T., p. 149), and draws attention to the importance of speculation in the valuation of investments on the Stock Exchange. Keynes's conclusion is, however, that:

after giving full weight to the importance of the influence of short-period changes in the state of long-term expectation as distinct from changes in the rate of interest, we are still entitled to return to the latter as exercising, at any rate, in normal circumstances, a great, though not a decisive, influence on the rate of investment (G.T., p. 164).

There are economists who have placed great stress on Keynes's treatment of uncertainty and expectations both in his treatment of investment and in his discussion of the demand for money. These views will be discussed more fully in the next chapter, when it will be argued that uncertainty plays an important role in Keynes's explanation of the interest-sensitivity of the demand for money, and this can be incorporated into the overall interpretation of the General Theory presented in this book. However, it will also be argued that there are no grounds for singling out Keynes's treatment of these topics for special attention.

This completes the analysis of Keynes's treatment of the consumption and investment functions. Having argued that investment depends upon the rate of interest, Keynes's next step is, obviously, an analysis of interest rate determination; this will be discussed in the next chapter. As Keynes's views on interest rate determination are closely linked with his views on money and uncertainty, these latter topics will also be discussed in the next chapter.

NOTE

1 Leijonhufvud, in particular, has emphasized Keynes's discussion of the windfall effect and quotes the following passage: 'Windfall changes in capital-values ... should be classified amongst *the major factors* capable of causing *short-period* changes in the propensity to consume' (G.T., pp. 92-3; quoted in Leijonhufvud, 1968, p. 191). However, it should be noted that it is on the propensity to consume and not on consumption, that the windfall effect is assumed to act, and Keynes, as already noted, regarded changes in the propensity to consume as having a secondary influence on consumption. So the windfall effect, by having a major impact on something which is no more than a secondary influence, presumably has nothing more than a secondary influence on consumption.

5   Money, Interest and Uncertainty

The main aim of this chapter is to concentrate on Keynes's analysis of the determination of the interest rate. The topics of money and uncertainty are particularly relevant in this context, and hence the overall relevance of these factors in Keynesian economics, as well as other contributions which have been made in this area, will be discussed here.

PART I

In his chapter 13, Keynes outlines his own theory of the rate of interest. He criticizes the classical theory in chapter 14, and chapter 15 is devoted to a more detailed exposition of his theory of the demand for money, which underlies his theory of how the interest rate is determined.

So far, Keynes has argued that investment will take place until the marginal efficiency of capital is equated to the interest rate. The next step, obviously, seems to be an analysis of the factors which determine the interest rate.

Keynes argues that there are two decisions which the individual, in deciding between present and future consumption, needs to take. There is, first of all, the question of how much of his present income to consume and therefore how much to save. Then, the further question arises, of what form the individual's saving should take; how much of this increment to his wealth should he leave in a relatively liquid form, and how much should he commit to more long-term saving? Keynes argues that the rate of interest is primarily relevant in influencing the second decision, in contrast to the classical theory, according to which it is primarily relevant in influencing the first decision. (Although the individual does have two distinct decisions to make, we should recognize that they are interdependent; factors which affect one may well affect the other as well). He writes: 'the rate of interest is the reward for parting with liquidity for a specified period' (G.T., p. 167) and argues that the classical theory of the rate of interest is mistaken in regarding it primarily as a factor which will influence the choice between present and future consumption. Although Keynes proceeds to a more detailed critique of the classical theory of interest in his next chapter, he states that it seems fairly obvious that the rate of interest cannot be the reward for waiting or saving as such, for someone who hoards his savings in cash would save just as much as someone who held interest-bearing assets, although he would earn no interest. He regards interest as 'a measure of the unwillingness of those who possess money to part with their liquid control of it' (G.T., p. 167). The rate of interest is the price which adjusts to equilibrate the desired holding of wealth in the form of cash with the actual available supply of it.

This gives rise to the problem of explaining why people should desire to hold their wealth in a non-interest bearing form. Keynes argues that the explanation necessarily involves uncertainty: uncertainty about the future of the rate of interest. Indeed, it will be argued in this chapter that uncertainty is primarily important in the General Theory inasmuch as it serves to underpin the speculative demand for money function and hence justifies an interest-sensitive demand for money. He gives several reasons why uncertainty might be relevant. In a certain world, people who foresaw a need for cash at a certain point of time in the future could buy a bond and then sell it again at an appropriate date in the future and 'If the current rate of interest is positive for debts of every maturity, it must always be more advantageous to purchase a debt than to hold cash as a store of wealth' (G.T., p. 169). However, in an uncertain world, this may not be so; there may be cases where an individual, wanting to obtain cash, would have to sell his securities at a loss. Depending on the probability of this occurring, the holding of cash over the period in question may be a more desirable alternative.[1] A second reason concerns the fact that there is likely to be a difference of opinion between people on the likely course of the interest rate. Someone whose views differ from the market's may hold cash in order to profit if bond prices move in the direction he anticipates they might. This is the essence of the explanation normally given for the speculative demand for money. It seems that Keynes concentrated on the speculative argument for the dependence of the demand for money on the interest rate; subsequently arguments have been given for expecting the transactions demand for money to depend on the interest rate (see, for example, Baumol, 1952, which concentrates on the role played by transactions costs). So Keynes has, in his chapter 13, introduced his own theory of the interest rate and criticized that of his predecessors, but only in a preliminary way. His next two chapters contain much more detailed analyses of both these questions.

Chapter 14 contains a more detailed critique of the classical theory of the rate of interest and it is only here that he states the classical theory fully. It is that 'Investment represents the demand for investible resources and saving represents the supply, whilst the rate of interest is the "price" of investible resources at which the two are equated' (G.T., p. 175). Keynes emphasizes that there seems to be no clear or explicit account of the theory in the writings of the classical school, but argues that the above seems to be a fairly clear statement of what lay behind their thinking on these matters, and he produces a fair amount of textual evidence to support this interpretation. Moreover, Keynes is in the advantageous position of once having been a classical economist: 'his theory seems to be this, and it is what I myself was brought up on and what I taught for many years to others' (G.T., p. 175). This is something which perhaps ought to be remembered when we are tempted to criticize Keynes as misrepresenting the classical economists; Keynes was attacking a position which he had held, believed in and taught for a number of years. The theory can be depicted as in Fig. 5.1. In equational form, it is given by the classical system equation introduced earlier in this book as equation (1.5):

$$C(Y, i) + I(i) = Y$$

with the additional premiss that income is at its full employment level. By using the definition of saving, it can be written in the form

$$I(i) = Y - C(Y, i) = S(Y, i)$$

In the Keynesian system, this equation instead becomes the national income equilibrium condition.

Keynes attacks the classical theory on the grounds that it is incompatible with the theory which he has so far developed for the determination of the level of output and employment. Suppose the level of investment changes; then in the aggregate supply and demand framework which has been developed, the level of income will also change. If it is assumed that the level of income is an argument of the savings function, then there will be a shift in the savings function. So a movement along one of the curves, the II curve, results in a bodily shift of the other, the SS curve. Hence, one of the presuppositions of partial equilibrium analysis, that the curves should be independent of each other, does not hold, and the analysis cannot be used to determine the rate of interest, given the Keynesian aggregate demand framework which has so far been developed in the book. The analysis does have the limited value that it enables the *full employment* rate of interest to be determined.

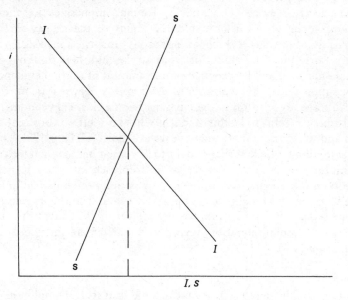

FIGURE 5.1

This will be the case if the SS curve can be taken to represent the amount that is saved out of the full employment level of income. But it does not enable us to determine the rate of interest in a disequilibrium context, where income is not necessarily at its full employment level, and where the rate of investment is one of the determinants of the level of income. As Keynes writes:

The classical theory of the rate of interest seems to suppose that, if the demand curve for capital shifts or if the curve relating the amount saved out of a given income shifts or if both these curves shift, the new rate of interest will be given by the point of intersection of the new positions of the two curves. But this is a nonsense theory. For the assumption that income is constant is incompatible with the assumption that these two curves can shift independently of one another. If either of them shift, then, in general, income will change; with the result that the whole schematism based on the assumption of a given income breaks down (G.T., p.179).

Perhaps Keynes is too severe in describing the classical theory of the interest rate as a 'nonsense theory' for there is nothing wrong with it, given the assumption underlying the classical theory; *given* the assumption that full employment is continuously maintained, it is a very plausible theory of the determination of the interest rate. However, given the theory of output and employment which Keynes has so far developed, the theory is invalid; the Keynesian aggregate demand theory is incompatible with the classical theory of the interest rate. Hence it becomes necessary for him to construct a new theory of the interest rate. This involves the role of the interest rate as an argument of the demand for money function, and will be considered in more depth in due course.

Perhaps it would be relevant here to relate Keynes's criticisms of the classical theory to the algebraic representation of the classical system we have given earlier on page 4. With the relaxation of the labour market clearing assumption, income is no longer constant when we come to consider equation (1.5), and hence the diagrammatic depiction of its determination no longer holds. The interest rate and the level of income will be determined by the whole simultaneous system, including the money market equilibrium condition. In the classical system, the interest rate is determined independently of the money market; hence the dependence of the demand for money on the interest rate is, as far as the classical system is concerned, irrelevant. This can explain the classical system's relative neglect of interest as an argument of the money demand function and Keynes's emphasis on the dependence of this function on the interest rate.

Keynes also suggests that there are two further points at which the classical economists might have realised they were on the wrong track.

The first concerns the possibility that the effect of the rate of interest on the level of saving might be ambiguous. Hence the savings schedule and the investment schedule might not cross and therefore there would be no equilibrium rate of interest. This is just mentioned as a possibility. However, Klein interprets this as Keynes's major point of divergence from the classical theory: 'It is more likely than not that there will be no positive value of r which satisfies this equation' (Klein, 1966, p. 85). However, there seems to be no evidence that Keynes placed any weight on this consideration; he mentions it just as an additional possibility for suggesting that the classical economists ought to have been aware of the deficiencies of their theory of the interest rate. The position taken here is that the reason why the classical theory of the interest rate is invalid as far as Keynes is concerned is that it is incompatible with the analytical framework he has already constructed.

The second point which Keynes thought would have perplexed the classical theorists is that it had normally been supposed that an increase in the quantity of money would tend to reduce the rate of interest and this would seem to be incompatible with their theory of the interest rate. Various attempts have been made to repair the deficiency, involving concepts such as 'forced savings', but these did not seem to be particularly satisfactory attempts since 'no reason has been given why a change in the quantity of money should affect either the investment-demand schedule or the readiness to save out of a given income' (G.T., p. 182). Keynes concludes the chapter by writing:

The reader will readily appreciate that the problem here under discussion is a matter of the most fundamental theoretical significance and of overwhelming practical importance.... A decreased readiness to spend will be looked on in quite a different light, if, instead of being regarded as a factor which will, cet. par., increase investment, it is seen as a factor which will, cet. par., diminish employment' (G.T., pp. 184-5).

In the next chapter, Keynes outlines his theory of the demand for money. Much of the material of this chapter is familiar and forms the subject of textbook expositions of Keynes's theory of money. However, an exposition of this chapter will be valuable in that it will enable some of the components of the interpretation presented here to be better understood.

Keynes, as is well known, considered three motives for money holding: the transactions-motive (which he further subdivided into the income-motive and the business-motive), the precautionary-motive and the speculative-motive. Keynes's innovation in the theory of the demand for money is normally regarded to be his introduction of the speculative-motive. This is one point of the traditional interpretation of Keynes which will not be questioned here.

Keynes assumed that the amount of money required to satisfy the first two motives is dependent almost entirely on the level of money-income in the economy and that, although the rate of interest may be expected to have some influence on those components of the demand for money, 'This is likely to be a minor factor except where large changes in the cost of holding cash are in question' (G.T., p.196). However, the dependence of the speculative-motive on the rate of interest is much more important, and it is through the speculative-motive that changes in the money supply have their effect on the economic system. Keynes suggests that 'experience indicates that the aggregate demand for money to satisfy the speculative motive usually shows a continuous response to gradual changes in the rate of interest' (G.T., p. 197). Hence, by open market operations, the authorities can change and control the rate of interest by changing the quantity of money.

As already argued: 'uncertainty as to the future course of the rate of interest is the sole intelligible explanation of the type of liquidity preference L_2 which leads to the holding of cash M_2' (G.T., p.201). It is here that uncertainty plays a crucial role in Keynes's theory.

Although he stresses that what matters may not be the absolute level of the interest rate, but its divergence from what might be considered to be a fairly safe level of the interest rate, there are still reasons, bound up with uncertainty, for thinking that a fall in the interest rate will result in an increase in the speculative demand for money.

The first concerns inelastic expectations of the 'safe' interest rate — 'if the general view as to what is a safe level of r is unchanged, every fall in r reduces the market rate relative to the 'safe' rate and therefore increases the risk of illiquidity' (G.T., p. 202) — and the second is a fairly ingenious argument concerning the insurance premium which interest provides against capital losses. If the rate of interest is very low, then this will offset only a very small expected fall in bond prices, whereas a higher interest rate will provide a greater degree of insurance: 'This, indeed, is perhaps the chief obstacle to a fall in the rate of interest to a very low level' (G.T., p. 202). The reasons presented here for expecting an interest sensitive demand for money function are slightly different from and complement the reasons given in chapter 13. However, all the arguments concern uncertainty; Keynes has presented a complex of reasons for thinking that the demand for money should be sensitive to the interest rate, and these all involve uncertainty. These arguments entail both that the rate of interest may under certain circumstances be fairly stable and also that it may be difficult to reduce the rate of interest below a certain level. What is crucial to Keynes's theory is that the interest rate should affect the demand for money and uncertainty is the reason he gives for thinking that it should. Here we might distinguish between Keynes's discussion of the reasons why the demand for money might depend upon the interest rate and his discussion of the precise form the dependence might take. As we have already argued, Keynes's basic divergence from the classical theory was his relaxation of the labour market clearing assumption and his postulation of an exogenous money wage. This change has, however, implications for the interpretation of other components of the system, and in particular leads us to emphasize the dependence of consumption on income and of the demand for money on the interest rate. Discussion of these topics we might characterize as discussion of important components of Keynes's theoretical structure which relate to the way in which it differs from the classical system. However, there is also discussion in the General Theory of particular components of his theoretical structure, which is not comparative in purpose and hence does not relate in any essential way to Keynes's divergence from the classical theory. Examples of such discussion are his discussion of the stability or instability of the investment function and his discussion of the interest-elasticity of the demand for money. Such discussions are relevant when the Keynesian theory is actually used for analyzing economic problems, but are not important inasmuch as the divergence between the Keynesian and the classical system is concerned. The position to be taken here concerning the liquidity trap, for example, is that Keynes believed in the possibility of a liquidity trap, but that this in no way constituted a reason for diverging from the classical system. His arguments against the classical theory and his alternative theoretical structure would be identical even had he not mentioned the possibility of a liquidity trap.

The next part of this chapter will discuss chapters 16 and 17 of the General Theory. These chapters may be somewhat of a detour which could be omitted without sacrificing the main argument (see Hansen, 1953, p. 155) but are also worth analyzing for their treatment of a number of issues. Having done this, the next part of the chapter will concentrate on analyzing Keynes's views on the liquidity trap. This to some extent follows on from earlier discussion in this chapter. Then some other interpretations of Keynes's views on money, interest and uncertainty will be considered, and particular attention will be given to those writers who attribute a much greater role to uncertainty in the structure of Keynes's theory than that presented here.

PART II

Chapter 16 is entitled 'Sundry Observations on the Nature of Capital'. Only the first section seems to be interesting from the exegetical point of view. There ideas are expressed quite widely in discussions of Keynes; it seems that these remarks are not intended as a justification of Keynes's theoretical structure, but are intended to make the theory and the novel ideas presented in the book appear plausible and fairly intuitive.

The basic idea presented in the first section of the chapter is that an act of saving may be undertaken in order to increase consumption in the future, but there is no reason why it should lead the productive resources, which otherwise would have been used to produce for present consumption, to be employed in preparing for future consumption. If anything, the reverse is likely to be the case, since expectations of future expenditure are likely to be influential in their effect on current investment. Hence, 'there should be nothing paradoxical in the conclusion that a diminished propensity to consume has, *cet. par.*, a depressing effect on employment' (G.T., p. 211).

This is sufficient to make intuitive and plausible Keynes's views on output and employment, but we should not regard it as in any way a rigorous argument for his conclusions. The possibility that other types of adjustment processes might take place is not considered. For example, he does not consider the possibility that there might be adjustment in the labour market or that the interest rate might move in order to restore a level of investment equal to full employment saving. So he does not produce a rigorous argument for the possibility of an underemployment equilibrium; it is a 'sundry observation' designed to make his views seem more plausible. The remainder of the chapter contains nothing of importance for our purpose. Therefore, Keynes's chapter 17, 'The Essential Properties of Interest and Money', will be next considered. This is perhaps one of the most puzzling chapters of the General Theory where 'certain deeper perplexities' are considered.

Keynes introduces chapter 17 with the remark that the rate of interest on money plays a special role in his theory of employment. His purpose in the chapter is to enquire why this should be so: it is a speculative enquiry into the nature of money and why a monetary economy should behave in the way it does. As such, it does not constitute an essential part of Keynes's theory; it might be possible for other foundations to his theoretical structure to be given, without invalidating the theoretical structure itself.

Keynes reminds us that the rate of interest is 'nothing more than the percentage excess of a sum of money contracted for forward delivery, e.g. a year hence, over what we may call the "spot" or cash price of the sum thus contracted for forward delivery' (G.T., p. 222) and therefore there is no reason why the concept of the rate of interest should not be applied to any capital asset, so that one could have a wheat rate of interest or a house rate of interest, for example. These interest rates could be measured in terms of the product itself, in terms of money or indeed in terms of any other product — for clarification on this, see Lerner (1952). These will differ by the appreciation or depreciation of the commodities' prices relative to each other. Henceforth, assets' returns as measured in a common currency will be compared. So, there are a large number of rates of interest; the problem now is that of explaining why the volume of output and employment 'is more intimately bound up with the money rate of interest than with the wheat rate of interest or the house rate of interest' (G.T., p. 225).

As a first step towards answering this question, Keynes lists the various returns which assets are likely to possess. There is, first of all, the yield or output which an asset is likely to produce (q), secondly the carrying cost (c) which is a measure of the wastage or the cost incurred through the mere passage of time in holding the asset and thirdly, the liquidity premium (l) attaching to the asset.

The rate of return on a commodity will be equal to $q - c + l$ (measured in terms of itself) and measured in terms of money it will be equal to this plus the expected appreciation of the asset. Since wealth holders' demands will be directed towards those assets the return on which is highest there will be a tendency for the returns to be driven to equality with one another. The return on an asset will be related to its demand-price, and those assets for which the demand-price exceeds the supply-price will be newly produced. As the stock of an asset increases, its demand-price will tend to fall and eventually a situation will be reached when, as long as the rate of interest does not fall, it will not be profitable to produce any more assets. Hence, Keynes suggests, if there is an asset, on which the rate of return tends to fall more slowly as output increases than on any other, this will tend to knock out the profitable production of all the other assets. It is suggested that there are several reasons why money is likely to be this asset, and hence why money is likely to cause problems in the economy.

The first property which Keynes considers is crucial is that money has a zero, or at least a very low, elasticity of production. By this he means that when the price of money rises (that is, the general price level falls) relative to the money-wage, extra resources are not devoted to producing more money. This is relevant for two reasons. First, the fact that money is not producible means that as the rates of return on other assets decline relative to money, and hence the output of these assets declines, this is not offset by an increased production of money and therefore aggregate demand falls. But secondly, this is a reason why the return on money does not tend to fall as the stocks of assets in general increase. For the reason why it was assumed that the rate of return on other assets would decline was because the stock of these increased, and hence this led to a lower rate of return. This possibility is no longer open in the case of money, and hence its rate of return is not likely to decline with that of other assets as output in general increases. However, this condition is insufficient to single money out for special attention, according to Keynes, since this condition is satisfied for all 'pure rent factors'. The second relevant property of money in this context is one it has in virtue of its being the medium of exchange and 'is that it has an elasticity of substitution equal to or nearly equal to zero, which means that as the exchange value of money rises, there is no tendency to substitute some other factor for it' (G.T., p. 231). This seems to be an incorrect argument. As the price level changes, then, *ceteris paribus*, the quantity of real balances agents want to hold may be assumed to stay constant. However, if this is true, the quantity of nominal balances they want to hold will certainly change and in proportion to the change in the price level. So an increase in the price of money (equivalently, a fall in the general price of commodities) will lead to a fall in desired money holdings. One would expect people to try to achieve this by substituting non-monetary assets for money. So Keynes's second point in this context seems to be based on a confusion between nominal and real balances. Therefore, money seems to be relevant only inasmuch as it is a non-reproducible store of value, and, as such, has nothing to distinguish it from other non-reproducible stores of value, such as land. The relevance of this will be discussed in due course. The third set of considerations which Keynes adduces in this context concerns whether these conclusions need to be modified at all when note is taken of the fact that the effective quantity of money can be increased by price level reductions. Keynes suggests that there are several reasons for thinking that this will not allow an adequate fall in the rate of interest. The first reason is that a fall in prices may, by inducing expectations of further falls in prices, reduce the rates of return obtainable on non-monetary assets, and therefore even if it does induce a fall in the interest rate the fall may not be adequate, since it is the difference between the rates of return on these assets and the money of interest which is relevant. The second reason is that money-wages may be sticky in terms of money, so that it may not be possible to engineer a sufficient decline in the money-wage rate. Keynes, moreover, suggests that this might have something to do with money's liquidity properties. The third point concerns the liquidity trap:

in certain circumstances, such as will often occur ... the rate of interest [will] be insensitive, particularly below a certain figure, even to a substantial increase in the quantity of money in proportion to other forms of wealth (G.T., p. 233).

So even if it is possible to induce a substantial downwards movement of the price level, and even if this does not have adverse consequences for the marginal efficiency of other assets, it may still not be possible to reduce the rate of interest below a certain level and hence changing the effective quantity of money via price level changes may not be an effective way of boosting output. Here, the low carrying costs of money are important — for only in the case of an asset with low carrying costs will a 'small stimulus ... due to the advantages of liquidity' (G.T., p. 233) lead to a large increase in the quantity of the asset held. So the liquidity trap may arise because money's return from the liquidity services it provides may not fall as its quantity increases, whereas there is no deterrent to the holding of a large quantity of money in the form of high (or rising) carrying costs.

We are therefore presented with the following picture of an economy: there are a number of assets in the economy, some reproducible, some non-reproducible. The rates of return on all the different assets will tend to equality with each other. Assets will be produced if their demand price is greater than their supply price; hence asset stocks will change and this will react on the rates of return. An asset may provide a barrier to the expansion of output if its rate of return does not tend to fall as output increases, and if this asset is non-reproducible. Money has these properties, and hence the money rate of interest may be crucial in setting a limit to the expansion of output. Money is crucial here inasmuch as it is a non-reproducible store of value. It is not the only non-reproducible store of value; Keynes suggests that there were perhaps times in the past when land may have created the same problems as money. However, it might be suggested that land is unlikely to create problems as frequently as money; money is universally held, whereas land is not; there may be heavy transactions costs involved in buying and selling land and land may not be so easily divisible as money. These conclusions are not offset by the fact that the effective quantity of money may be increased if the price level is flexible downwards. Hence, money in Keynes is important for a number of reasons; it is a non-reproducible store of value; its return consists almost entirely of the liquidity services which it provides, but it has negligible carrying costs. All these factors interact in a cumulative fashion to create the problems which money causes in the economy. (This is not to deny that money may enable real resources to be saved by enabling some of the resources which would otherwise be devoted to barter to be reduced. But money may create problems of its own.)

In conclusion, the following points are perhaps worth making in assessing Keynes's views as expressed in chapter 17. The first point to make is that these views are speculative and in no way presuppose or underlie the rest of Keynes's theoretical construction. Secondly, the reasons given for attributing importance to money are complex and depend upon the interaction of a number of factors. Thirdly, his views, although interesting and profound, are not entirely correct. We have drawn attention to Keynes's confusion between nominal and real balances on page 231 of the General Theory (and we have already argued that Keynes's argument against Fisher's distinction between the nominal and the real interest rate on page 142 loses some of its force if the distinction between nominal and real balances is made). Lerner draws our attention to some other mistakes in the chapter; at one point Keynes seems to confuse an equilibrium condition with an identity (Lerner, 1952, pp. 181-2) and at another point he seems to confuse stability and stickiness (*ibid.*, p. 186).

PART III

The next topic to be considered is the role of the liquidity trap in Keynes's General Theory. This has already been mentioned in the discussion of his theory of the demand for money; but since the extent of Keynes's belief in the liquidity trap, and the question of whether he mentions it at all in the General Theory have been controversial issues, some clarification on these points might be helpful.

There are a number of passages in the book which suggest that Keynes considered the possibility that the demand for money might become highly, or even infinitely elastic with respect to the interest rate at some specific interest rate.

Here it will be argued that his views on the possibility of a liquidity trap are considerably more subtle than is often made out to be the case; hence a fairly careful analysis of his views on these issues seems justified.

Keynes first mentions the possibility of a liquidity trap in chapter 13, where he is introducing his theory of the rate of interest: 'circumstances can develop in which even a large increase in the quantity of money may exert a comparatively small influence on the rate of interest' (G.T., p. 172). Two reasons are given for this. The second is the argument normally given for the liquidity trap: 'opinion about the future of the rate of interest may be so unanimous that a small change in present rates may cause a mass movement into cash' (*ibid.*). This provides support for Tobin's interpretation of Keynes's theory of liquidity preference (see Tobin 1958, pp. 67-9). The other reason is that a large increase in the quantity of money may increase uncertainty about the future so that the precautionary or security motive for holding cash is increased. Here, a movement along the liquidity preference schedule causes it to move outwards. This is evidence that Keynes considered the liquidity preference schedule to be highly unstable.

The next discussion of these issues comes in chapter 15, where Keynes has proceeded to a more detailed analysis of the theory of the demand for money. He makes the point that 'what matters is not the absolute level of r, but the degree of its divergence from what is considered to be a fairly safe level of r (G.T., p. 201) and a few pages later, reinforces this with 'any level of interest which is accepted with sufficient conviction as likely to be durable will be durable' (G.T., p. 203). So here he emphasizes that the interest rate is likely to be quite sticky around its current level. However, there are qualifications; these problems are particularly likely to arise when a monetary policy is being pursued 'which strikes public opinion as being experimental in character or easily liable to change' (G.T., p. 203), but can be avoided if the authorities are prepared to pursue a sufficiently determined monetary policy.

Keynes also emphasizes that these considerations do not normally mean that an increase in the money supply (or more strictly, an increase in that portion of the money supply which is not required for transactions purposes) does not lead to a fall in interest rates. So although Keynes suggests that there may well be an element of rigidity in the interest rate, this is not likely to prove a decisive barrier to an expansionary monetary policy. He also suggests that there will be an obstacle to the fall of the interest rate to a very low level. This concerns the 'insurance premium' which the rate of interest provides. When the rate of interest is very low, it only requires a small expected capital loss on bonds to make the holding of bonds inferior to the holding of money. (This is a point made earlier.) Hence, this insurance effect is likely to prevent the falling of the rate of interest below a certain low level.

Keynes also discusses the relationship between the short-term interest rate and the long-term rate. He suggests that if open market operations are confined to the purchase of short-dated securities, the authorities may not be able to have much impact on the long-term rate of interest. This is a point which is mentioned in his discussion of the monetary authorities' ability 'to establish any given complex of rates of interest for debts of different terms and risks' (G.T., p. 203). Another point which is mentioned here is that it may be impossible to reduce long-term interest rates below a certain level because of the liquidity trap — and it is definitely the liquidity trap:

after the rate of interest has fallen to a certain level, liquidity preference may become virtually absolute in the sense that almost everyone prefers cash to holding a debt which yields so low a rate of interest . . . . But whilst this limiting case might become practically important in future, I know of no example of it hitherto (G.T., p. 207).

So here Keynes seems to dismiss the practical relevance of the liquidity trap. Another reason which might stand in the way of bringing the rate of interest below a certain figure is that there are 'the intermediate costs of bringing the borrower and the ultimate lender together' (G.T., p. 208). Hence Keynes in fact gives several reasons for thinking that there may be circumstances in which it might be impossible to reduce the rate of interest below a certain figure.

So Keynes, when discussing the demand for money, mentions but does not emphasize the liquidity trap. However, later in the book, he tends to give more emphasis to it. In his chapter on the 'Essential Properties of Interest and Money', he writes: 'in certain circumstances such as will often occur [the characteristics of money which satisfy liquidity] will cause the rate of interest to be insensitive, particularly below a certain figure, even to a substantial increase in the quantity of money in proportion to other forms of wealth' (G.T., p.233). Keynes emphasizes the liquidity trap here in a context in which it is expedient for him to do so; he needs a reason for thinking that an increase in the effective quantity of money via a price-level change will not alter the conclusions he has reached about the role of money in the economy (see earlier analysis of this chapter). Later, Keynes suggests that the liquidity trap might in fact be crucial in preventing monetary policy from enabling a return to full employment:

The most stable, and the least easily shifted, element in our contemporary economy has been hitherto, and may prove to be in future the minimum rate of interest acceptable to the generality of wealth owners. If a tolerable level of employment requires a rate of interest much below the average rates which ruled in the nineteenth century, it is most doubtful whether it can be achieved merely by manipulating the quantity of money (G.T., p.309).

So Keynes does seem to be inconsistent in the emphasis he places on the liquidity trap in the book. He tends to emphasize it more later on. Earlier, whilst he recognizes it as a possibility, he does not seem to consider that it poses an insuperable barrier to an expansionary monetary policy. Also, whilst his development of the theory of the speculative demand for money can be expected to lead fairly plausibly to the view that under certain circumstances the demand for money might become infinitely, or at least highly, elastic at some interest rate, Keynes does not rely solely on speculative factors to underpin the liquidity trap. For example, there is the 'insurance premium' argument and the idea that the costs of bringing lenders and borrowers together should create a floor to the interest rate.

There is sufficient evidence, therefore, that Keynes did believe in the possibility of a liquidity trap, but did not believe that this in any way constituted an important divergence from the classical theory. Evidence is provided for this in chapter 18 when he sums up his General Theory. There he does not mention the liquidity trap, although he does mention the liquidity preference schedule and its dependence on the rate of interest. Having summarized the General Theory, Keynes writes:

But the actual phenomena of the economic system are also coloured by certain special characteristics of the propensity to consume, the schedule of the marginal efficiency of capital and the rate of interest, about which we can safely generalize from experience, but which are not logically necessary (G.T., p. 249).

Here Keynes seems to be making the type of distinction we have tried to make above — the distinction between those components of Keynes's book which relate to his divergence from the classical theory and those which relate to specific components of his theory but which are not essentially comparative in nature; according to the interpretation presented here, Keynes's views on the liquidity trap, as well as those on the volatility of the investment function, are to be placed in the latter category, and hence are not points of divergence from the classical theory.

PART IV

In this section, the relevance of some later work on the significance of uncertainty will be discussed.

The view has sometimes been expressed that Keynes laid great, indeed crucial stress on uncertainty and that his divergence from the classical school consisted of his recognition of the implications of uncertainty. Shackle in particular has taken this point of view, and the position is well summarized by Loasby: '... unemployment in a market economy is the result of ignorance too great to be borne. The fully specified macro-economic models miss the point — which is precisely that no model of this situation can be fully specified.' (Loasby, 1976, p. 167). Shackle, in discussing Keynes's General Theory writes: 'A book which concludes by difficult and entangled steps that stable curves and functions are allergic to the real human scheme of things proceeded to state this idea in terms of stable curves or functions' (Shackle, 1973, pp. 517-8). We can perhaps distinguish two versions of this view: a more extreme version, according to which the implications of uncertainty are argued to have consequences generally destructive of economic theory and a more moderate version, according to which uncertainty, in its implications for investment and the demand for money, is of crucial importance in explaining short-term economic movements and thus constitutes Keynes's crucial departure from the classical theory.

These views are inconsistent with the interpretation which is presented in this book. Here it is argued that uncertainty is important in Keynes's theoretical structure primarily inasmuch as it underpins the speculative demand for money function, and the associated interest-sensitivity of the demand for money. It will not be disputed that Keynes believed the marginal efficiency of capital schedule to be fickle and unstable. However, the position to be taken here is that he did not consider this to be in any way a point of divergence from the classical theory.

It will be argued here that the evidence cited by the above writers in no way supports their thesis and that there are several pieces of evidence against their thesis. It should be noted that it is admitted by Shackle that this thesis is by no means clear and Loasby describes the above conclusion as 'fearfully obscure', at least as far as the General Theory is concerned. However, several pieces of evidence are presented in favour of this interpretation. The major piece of evidence is Keynes's *Quarterly Journal of Economics* article (Keynes, 1937a). Sometimes chapter 12 and chapter 17 of the General Theory are also cited in support of this position.

It is certainly true that Keynes's 1937 article does contain a long section on the precariousness of our views of the future and the flimsiness of the evidence upon which we base our decisions. However, the implications of this are argued to be that the classical theory of interest was 'a mistaken theory of the rate of interest' (Keynes, 1937a, p. 224). When discussing a classical economist's failure to recognize the full implications of uncertainty, he writes: 'I think he has overlooked the precise nature of the difference which his abstraction makes between theory and practice ... this is particularly the case in his treatment of money and interest' (*ibid.*, p. 218). So Keynes certainly emphasizes the nature of uncertainty in this article, but also argues that its implications are likely to be almost entirely related to the theory of the interest rate, which is the interpretation presented in this book. Many of the other components of the theory are introduced in the article, so the article presents no evidence in favour of the view that uncertainty leads to nihilistic conclusions about economic theory. Keynes mentions the fact that investment 'should fluctuate widely from time to time' (*ibid.*, p. 220) but no reason is given for thinking that this fact is of crucial importance inasmuch as his divergence from the classical theory is concerned. So the Keynes (1937a) article provides very little support for the Loasby/Shackle interpretation of Keynes. Little support is provided by the two chapters sometimes cited in favour of this point of view, chapters 12 and 17. As we have argued, Keynes did not regard his investment theory as in any way a divergence from the classical theory, and he concludes his chapter with the following remarks: 'we are still entitled to return to the [rate of interest] as exercising a great, though not decisive, influence on the rate of investment' (G.T., p. 164).

There are several pieces of evidence which can be presented against this interpretation. First, Hicks's 1937 article on 'Mr. Keynes and the Classics' (Hicks, 1937), of which Keynes wrote that he had 'next to nothing to say by way of criticism' (see Hicks, 1973, p. 9), contains virtually nothing on the implications of uncertainty. Secondly, when Keynes is led to summarize the General Theory in chapter 18 (see G.T., pp. 245-9), he does not in any way emphasize the volatility of the marginal efficiency of capital schedule. He does write: 'there is not one of the above factors which is not liable to change without much warning, and sometimes substantially' (G.T., p. 249). This could certainly include instability of the marginal efficiency of capital schedule, but no reason is given for focussing on this. Thirdly, Keynes's book contains many equilibrium conditions, for example, the real wage is equated to the marginal product of labour and the marginal efficiency of capital is equated to the interest rate. This seems to constitute a decisive objection to the view that Keynes's treatment of uncertainty led him to generally nihilistic conclusions about economic theory.

The conclusion I would draw is that the Shackle/Loasby interpretation of Keynes has little, if anything, in it.

Another view concerning Keynes and uncertainty which has gained currency in recent years, particularly in the writings of Leijonhufvud, is that Keynes's crucial divergence from the Classics was the removal of the Walrasian auctioneer[2] and the associated tâtonnement process. Leijonhufvud takes this view: 'To make the transition from Walras' world to Keynes' world, it is thus sufficient to dispense with the assumed tâtonnement mechanism' (Leijonhufvud, 1967, p. 301).

There are several points to be made in connection with this point of view. First, it might be argued that the rigorous study of non-tâtonnement adjustment processes does not seem to have produced unambiguously Keynesian conclusions; in fact, no very definite conclusions seem to have emerged, so one can hardly say that to reach Keynes's world it is *sufficient* to dispense with the tâtonnement mechanism. It may be more plausible to argue that in order to make the jump it is necessary to dispense with the tâtonnement mechanism — inasmuch as tâtonnement guarantees market-clearing equilibria, it would seem to be necessary to relax the tâtonnement requirement in order to reach a non-market clearing equilibrium. However, this conclusion is by no means clear; examples have been given of unstable tâtonnement processes — for example, Scarf (1960).

Secondly, there is no evidence at all that Keynes had Walras's theory in mind when attacking the classical theory, or even that he was familiar with the bare essentials of Walras' theory when writing the General Theory. The only reference to Walras in the General Theory is one to his capital theory on pages 176-7, and is basically designed to show that Walras, at least in his treatment of capital theory, was an adherent of classical economics. The classical theory Keynes was attacking is outlined in chapter 1 of this book; its assumption that markets cleared could be based on the belief that the adjustment process in markets was equilibrating (as argued in chapter 2) and need not be based on a more stringent belief in the existence of an auctioneer.

Thirdly, this view sheds no light on the specific structure of the General Theory in which just one market, the labour market, fails to clear. If Leijonhufvud's were a correct interpretation of Keynes, then we would expect all markets to fail to clear, not just the labour market. Leijonhufvud gives no reason for thinking that the labour market should be any different from any other market. There seems to be no indication that the classical economists, as depicted by Keynes, relied on any tâtonnement process to justify their theory. As discussed in chapter 2, an argument that the adjustment process in each market was equilibrating could under certain circumstances justify the use of equilibrium analysis as, at least, a useful simplification for some types of analysis. Keynes singled the labour market out for attention because he thought that this argument was not valid in the case of the labour market; his arguments had nothing to do with the absence or presence of any supposed tâtonnement adjustment mechanisms.

PART V

In this section, various views on the role of money in the economy and the significance of the economy's being a monetary one will be considered. As argued earlier, Keynes believed that the reasons why money was important were fairly complex, and depended upon an interaction between the fact that money is a non-reproducible store of value and its liquidity properties. Various other views have been expressed on the nature and role of money. Here the contributions these views make towards our understanding of Keynesian theory will be assessed and the significance of the economy's being a monetary economy will be discussed.

The first view to be considered is Clower's dictum, 'Money buys goods and goods buy money; but goods do not buy goods' (Clower, 1967, pp. 207-8). This, at face value seems to be nothing more than a statement of money's function as a medium of exchange and as such nothing of significance flows from it. However, a number of arguments have been based on the role of money as a medium of exchange, and some of these will be reviewed here. The reason why the Clower dictum has been held to be of significance is perhaps that it has been confused with his dual decision hypothesis, and the suggestion has arisen that this in some way presupposes a monetary economy. As has been argued in chapter 4, this is not so; the dual decision hypothesis and money's role as a medium of exchange are discussed in different articles — the dual decision hypothesis features in Clower (1965), whereas Clower's dictum appears in Clower (1967). The dual decision hypothesis, which states that when an agent is constrained in one market, his demands in other markets will be affected, in no way presupposes a monetary economy; it is simply a consequence of utility maximization subject to a budget constraint and an additional quantity constraint; nowhere in the analysis need it be presupposed that the economy is a monetary one.

However, Leijonhufvud has an argument based on money's role as a medium of exchange which goes somewhat as follows: in a monetary economy, the fact that trade must be mediated by money means that suppliers of labour, who have an excess supply of labour and a corresponding (notional) excess demand for goods, cannot 'communicate' their excess demand for goods to producers and hence the excess supply of labour will persist. However, in a barter economy, it is argued, this problem will not arise; excess demands will be communicated (see Leojonhufvud, 1968, pp. 89-91). This argument was discussed in chapter 2, where it was argued that the firm should employ exactly the same criterion in the barter case as in the money case, and therefore that the argument does not work.

Grossman, however, in a comment on an article by Leijonhufvud (see Grossman, 1974) has a different argument for the significance of the monetisation of exchange. He considers a model, which seems to be a special case of the Barro-Grossman fixed price model (see Barro-Grossman, 1976), where gold initially serves as a medium of exchange, and where households exchange labour services for commodities; firms by employing labour services, produce commodities. He considers the difference made by making commodities the medium of exchange. The lesson seems to be that an excess supply of the medium of exchange cannot co-exist with an excess supply of commodities: in that case, the excess supply of the medium of exchange would be eliminated by being spent on commodities. Hence the monetization of exchange will have certain implications for the possible combinations of excess supplies and demands in the economy. But this argument does not seem to touch the Keynesian problem of whether there can be an excess supply of labour or not. (The arguments in the following section will also be relevant in assessing the foregoing points.)

The final argument, or set of arguments concerning the role of money in the economy which will be considered here are those produced by Benassy. In a series of papers, he has rigorously analyzed exchange under disequilibrium (that is, non-market clearing) conditions and has drawn some conclusions about the efficiency (or otherwise) of monetary and non-monetary economies (see Benassy, 1975). He argues that monetary economies will be characterized by a particular type of in-efficiency which will be absent from barter economies. (By a barter economy is meant an economy where every good is tradeable — at zero cost — against every other good. A pure monetary economy is one where there is one commodity — the monetary commodity — which is tradeable against every other commodity, but no two commodities are tradeable against each other if neither is the monetary commodity).

Benassy considers a fixed price model, where the prices are not the Walrasian (that is, general equilibrium) prices. Agents express demands on markets expecting that they will face various quantity constraints. The actual transactions they will realise in any market will depend upon the demands expressed by all agents in that market. An equilibrium will be that state of affairs where agents effect the transactions they expected to be able to undertake. Benassy shows that under certain conditions, an equilibrium of this type (which will almost certainly involve rationing or non-market clearing on most markets) will exist. He then proceeds to introduce an efficiency concept for such an economy: 'a state will be efficient if, at the given set of prices, no trades bearing on pairs of goods can improve, strictly, the utility of all traders involved' (*op. cit.*, p. 149).

He shows that a barter economy as defined above, will in general be efficient. However, this result will not hold for a monetary economy. Since all goods are not tradeable against all other goods, it may be possible to find sequences of exchange which, if feasible, would make everyone better off, but which cannot be undertaken, given the deficiency of markets. It is suggested that the sequence of utility improving pairwise exchanges might be referred to as a multiplier process, analogous to (or identical with?) the standard Keynesian multiplier.

The analysis is rigorous and correct; however, a number of comments seem to be relevant here on the significance of this work for understanding the role of money in the economy. First, as Benassy himself emphasizes, the various transactions costs associated with barter exchange and which impel the development of a monetary economy are not considered or incorporated into the analysis at all. But this is something which must be considered if a comparison of the relative efficiencies of barter and monetary economies is to be made. Secondly, it is perhaps worthwhile pointing out that the result produced by Grossman referred to earlier is the type of result which could have come out of a more specific version of the Benassy model. Changing the commodity which functions as a medium of exchange will change the pairwise exchange possibilities and this may lead to a change in the realised pattern of excess demands. Thirdly, and perhaps most importantly, the type of inefficiency analyzed by Benassy does not seem to be the same type of problem as that analyzed by Keynes. Benassy considers a fixed-price model where there may be an inefficiency due to the fact that all logically possible pairwise exchanges may not be able to be undertaken. Keynes considers a model where just the labour market fails to clear, and all other prices are flexible and equilibrate the relevant markets. Multiplier processes take place in this economy and labour either becomes more or less constrained as aggregate demand changes. Disequilibrium, however, will still occur in the Benassy model even in the pure barter case if prices are not the Walrasian ones. Hence it seems clear that the 'transactions structure' of the economy is not the only factor determining whether disequilibrium is present in the economy or not. It also seems clear that the disequilibrium that Keynes was concerned with was bound up with a misalignment of relative prices. He continually emphasized that an increase in employment would be associated with a decline in the real wage. So perhaps we can distinguish two types of reason for the existence and extent of disequilibrium. First, a wrong vector of prices. Secondly, an inappropriate transactions structure. The second reason presupposes the first: a necessary and sufficient condition for disequilibrium to occur is that prices are wrong. But given the first, the second may determine the spread and extent of disequilibrium. The position taken here is that Keynes was concerned with the first problem and Benassy with the second; hence the types of consideration that Benassy brings to bear on the second problem are not relevant in understanding Keynesian problems. It has certainly not been shown for example, that unemployment is impossible in a barter economy; this buttresses Hahn's conclusion on this issue (see Hahn, 1977, p. 31) and we may concur with his view that a false trail has been laid here; so far, the view that money as a medium of exchange is of crucial importance for Keynesian economics or for the possibility of an unemployment equilibrium has little, if anything, to commend in it. Of course, the analyses of Benassy are valuable, primarily in that they extend the application of rigorous techniques, formerly used in general equilibrium analysis to the behaviour of an economy in disequilibrium. The argument presented here is designed to show that they are of little consequence for Keynesian economics.

As argued earlier, the reasons why money is held by Keynes to be important are fairly complex. Money has a number of properties, and it is the interaction of these properties which is responsible for a monetary economy behaving in the way it does. But these reasons are speculative and do not underlie the rest of the theory.

So Keynes has by now built his theory of the workings of the economy with a non-clearing labour market. It remains to apply it to a number of problems, the most important of which will be the analysis of the effects of wage changes on output and employment. This, and other issues which Keynes discusses in the last part of the General Theory, will be discussed in the next chapter.

NOTES

1   This is Keynes's argument. However, it seems that this argument is not correct. If the interest rate is positive for debts of *every* maturity it would presumably be positive for debts of *zero* maturity (that is, sight deposits), and the holding of these will hence always be preferable to the holding of cash over the period in question. Even if the interest rate is positive only for debts of positive maturity, Keynes's argument is still incorrect in a model with a continuum of maturities and no transactions costs. (I am indebted to John Flemming for this point.)

2   The Walrasian auctioneer was the device introduced by Walras in order to enable equilibrium prices to be established. The auctioneer would announce a set of prices, economic agents would compute their demands and supplies at these prices and communicate them to the auctioneer, who would adjust the price vector depending upon whether there was excess supply or excess demand for goods. No trading would take place until an equilibrium price vector was reached. The process whereby the market 'groped' towards an equilibrium was described as a 'tâtonnement'.

6　Changes in Money-Wages

By the end of Book IV, Keynes has constructed his theory of employment and he restates it in chapter 18. The remainder of the book is devoted to applying the theory to a number of problems and to discussing some of the implications the theory might have. This chapter will concentrate on his chapter 19, where he considers the effects of money-wage changes on output and employment and on some of the literature the approach he takes here has inspired.

In constructing his theory, Keynes assumes an exogenous or parametric money-wage (see, for example, p. 247, where he regards 'the wage-unit, as determined by the bargains reached between employers and employees' as one of the theory's 'ultimate independent variables'). With his theory complete, he can explore the implications of changing this exogenous money-wage. As he notes, it is somewhat unfortunate that only at this point can he explore the implications of money-wage flexibility, since the classical theory he is combatting relies on the view that money-wage flexibility ensures a self-regulating economic system, and hence earlier discussions might have been helpful. But this was not possible before the development of his own theory.

A summary of Keynes's assumptions about money-wages may be useful at this point. First, as we have seen in our discussion of chapter 2, Keynes did not assume money-wage rigidity in constructing his theory and did not give it as his reason for rejecting the classical theory of employment. His major argument against the classical theory is that the adjustment behaviour in the labour market may not be equilibrating, and this justifies our constructing a model of the economy in which just the labour market fails to clear. Secondly, in actually constructing the theory, he regards the money-wage as exogenous. Thirdly, the theory can be used to analyse the effects of money-wage changes, once it has been developed, by considering changes in the parametric money-wage.

Keynes does not entirely disagree with the classical conclusion that a fall in money-wages will increase output and employment: 'A reduction in money-wages is quite capable in certain circumstances of affording a stimulus to output' (G.T., p. 257), but emphasizes that his difference from the classical theory is primarily one of analysis, not of conclusion. First of all, he outlines the classical arguments, then he presents his own.

However, it seems that the classical arguments have rarely, if ever, been stated precisely; this is not the only occasion Keynes has had reason to complain about the lack of clarity or precision of the classical economists in presenting their theory (see, for example, G.T., p. 175). So here Keynes is presenting what he takes to be the classical argument that a fall in money-wages will tend to increase output and employment. The argument seems to be nothing more than an elaboration of the idea that if money-wages fall, costs will fall; if costs fall prices will fall; if prices fall then there will be a movement along a demand curve; output and hence employment will increase. The argument is extended from the case of the individual industry to the whole economy. Commenting on this argument, Keynes writes: 'If this is the ground-work of the argument (and, if it is not, I do not know what the groundwork is), surely it is fallacious'. (G.T., p. 259) For the argument on the industrial level is constructed on the basis of *ceteris paribus* assumptions 'as to the nature of the demand and supply schedules of other industries and as to the amount of the aggregate effective demand' (*ibid.*), so when the argument is transferred from the industry level to the aggregate level, these assumptions must similarly be transferred. But then the extremely restrictive nature of the classical conclusion becomes apparent. For whilst it would not be denied that a reduction in money-wages, accompanied by the same aggregate effective demand as before (measured in terms of money) would increase output and employment, this is not the question at issue; the relevant question is whether the reduction will in fact be accompanied by a maintenance of aggregate effective demand. But the classical theory has no method of analyzing this question, and hence cannot answer the question as to what effect a fall in money-wages will have. So Keynes proceeds to apply his own theory to tackling the problem. To sum up on the classical argument on the effects of wage-reductions on employment: the classical theory has an argument according to which a fall in money-wages will increase employment, but this presupposes constant aggregate demand. If this last assumption cannot be granted (as, surely, it cannot), then the classical theory cannot analyze the effect money-wage reductions have on employment.

According to Keynes's theory, a change in money-wages (or in anything else, for that matter) can change employment only if it changes one of the factors underlying the effective demand schedule. Hence it can affect employment only if it has some sort of impact either on the propensity to consume, the marginal efficiency of capital schedule, or the rate of interest. Unless there is an impact on at least one of these factors, money-wage changes will not affect output and employment. Here Keynes seems to be using an aggregate supply curve defined in 'wage units', so that money-wage changes do not affect it. This enables Keynes to show the limitations of the view that a reduction in money-wages will increase employment 'because it reduces the cost of production'. Suppose that entrepreneurs expect a fall in money-wages will have this effect (this is the assumption most favourable to this point of view) and try to increase their output; then unless one of the three factors mentioned above is affected, entrepreneurs will be disappointed in the sales-proceeds they receive from their increased output and they will reduce their production to its original level. So an analysis of the effects of money-wage changes on output and employment requires a consideration of their effects on the three factors mentioned above. Keynes presents a taxonomy of possible effects which does not pretend to be comprehensive, but which is intended to include the most important effects. Here, the effects Keynes gives will be listed and discussed:

1 There may be income-distributional effects; wage earners

may suffer and those on a (relatively) fixed income may gain. This will affect the propensity to consume, and Keynes suggests that, on the balance of probabilities, the effect is likely to be adverse (that is, it is likely to reduce the propensity to consume).

2   There may be open economy effects, if the reduction in money-wages is a reduction relative to money-wages abroad. This may improve the balance of trade, and Keynes considers that this will improve investment. There are also effects on the terms of trade which perhaps ought to be considered.

3   There may be expectational effects which react on the marginal efficiency of capital. These effects could go in either direction, depending upon how expectations of future wages and prices are influenced. If the reduction in money-wages is a reduction relative to what is expected in the future, then the effect of the marginal efficiency of capital will be favourable. However, if the reduction is expected to herald further reductions, then the effect will be in the opposite direction. It will diminish the marginal efficiency of capital and tend to lead to a postponement of both investment and consumption. Another way of expressing the effect is to consider the distinction between real and nominal interest rates, alluded to earlier (see pp. 69–71). Suppose there is an expectation of a fairly steady rate of inflation or deflation. The appropriate investment decision will be based on a comparison between the marginal efficiency of capital and the interest rate. If the marginal efficiency of capital is measured in money terms (that is, the expected returns are discounted back to the present without an adjustment for inflation) then this should be compared with the nominal interest rate. If it is measured in real terms, so that expected future costs and prices are adjusted for expected changes in the value of money, then it should be compared with the real interest rate. This could lead to a state of affairs which is extremely unfavourable to investment. For whether or not there is a liquidity trap, the nominal rate of interest must always be above the zero nominal rate of return which can always be obtained by holding money. Hence the higher the rate of deflation the higher the real rate of interest must be. If the marginal efficiency of capital, measured in real terms, is invariant with respect to the rate of inflation or deflation, then the greater the rate of deflation, the higher the real interest rate might be expected to be, and hence the lower investment will be. For

example, if prices are expected to fall at an annual rate of 10 per cent then the real rate of return must be at least 11⅑ per cent, for that is the return which can be costlessly obtained by holding money[1]. So deflation may well be extremely unfavourable to aggregate demand, through its effects on investment, if it is expected to persist. It is basically this point Keynes is making when he writes: 'The most unfavourable contingency is that in which money-wages are slowly sagging downwards and each reduction in wages seems to diminish confidence in the prospective maintenance of wages' (G.T., p.265). The reverse argument, that inflation may be a 'good thing' because it tends to boost investment by reducing the real rate of interest, has sometimes been made.

4   There may be effects on the rate of interest. A general fall in wages and prices will, *ceteris paribus*, reduce the amount of cash required for transactions purposes; this will tend to reduce the rate of interest since more cash will be available to satisfy the speculative motive and hence the price of bonds will be bid up. But it is important to stress the *ceteris paribus* qualifications, for the fall in wages may, by disturbing political confidence, result in a rightward shift of the liquidity preference schedule.

5   There may be other expectational effects on entrepreneurs. They may react favourably to the fall in money-wages (if they mistakenly believe that the fall in money-wages is particularly advantageous to them), but this may be offset if workers make the same mistake as employers, and react unfavourably to the fall in money-wages. Another relevant point concerns the effects of indebtedness: 'Indeed, if the fall of wages and prices goes far, the embarrassment of those entrepreneurs who are heavily indebted may soon reach the point of insolvency — with severely adverse effects on investment' (G.T., p.264).

This basically summarizes Keynes's analysis of the effects of money-wage changes on output and employment. He writes: 'This is not a complete catalogue of all the possible reactions of wage reductions in the complex real world. But [they] cover, I think, those which are usually the most important' (G.T., p.264). One point worth making is that Keynes does not consider explicitly the effect that higher real balances might have on the propensity to consume either directly, or via their effect on the interest rate.

The upshot of the discussion is that if we confine our attention to a closed economy, and do not count on any favourable reaction from income distributional effects then money-wage reductions can only have a favourable effect on output through their effect either on the marginal efficiency of capital or on the interest rate. A situation in which money-wages are slowly declining is not likely to have a favourable effect on the marginal efficiency of capital. On the other hand, a large reduction where it is believed that the wage will then gradually increase may be much more favourable; however, it is extremely unlikely that such a reduction can be accomplished under a system of free wage bargaining. So there is little, if anything, to hope for from money-wage reductions inasmuch as repercussions on the marginal efficiency of capital are concerned. The conclusion of the discussion is therefore that 'it is on the effect of a falling wage and price level on the demand for money that those who believe in the self-adjusting quality of the economic system must rest the weight of their argument' (G.T., p. 266). It follows that a flexible wage policy can have the same effect on output and employment — and is subject to the same limitations — as monetary policy. If there are reasons why monetary policy alone cannot restore full employment under certain circumstances, then a flexible wage policy will similarly be unable to achieve that result.

However, although the policies may be analytically the same in their effect on output and employment since they are both ways of changing the quantity of money in terms of wage-units, there are other considerations which should influence the choice between them. Keynes mentions three relevant considerations. First, it is extremely difficult, if not impossible, to achieve a uniform reduction in wage rates, whereas it is relatively easy to change the quantity of money. Secondly, given that there are certain groups of incomes which are relatively fixed in terms of money, considerations both of social justice and of social expediency may entail that all factors should have incomes which are relatively inflexible in terms of money. Thirdly, there will be different effects on the burden of indebtedness. A fall in the wage unit may increase the burden of indebtedness and this may well be undesirable.

So, analytically, the effects of a policy of money-wage flexibility can be achieved equally well by a policy of monetary expansion; however, there are several compelling reasons for preferring the latter to the former. Keynes concludes: 'I am now of the opinion that the maintenance of a stable general level of money-wages is, on a balance of considerations, the most advisable policy for a closed system' (G.T., p.270). There is the additional point to make that in his conclusion, that the effects of money-wage reductions are basically the same as those of an expansionary monetary policy, Keynes has assumed that the various expectational effects which are likely to prove adverse to investment do not operate, or at least can be offset by an expansionary monetary policy; hence his conclusion, if anything, grants more than is strictly justifiable to a policy of money-wage reduction.

In chapter 19, Keynes has used his theoretical framework to analyze the effects changes in money-wages will have on output and employment. In subsequent chapters he deals with other issues; there is nothing in them which is particularly important as far as the interpretation given here is concerned, and the discussion of them will be brief.

The appendix to chapter 19 is devoted to a discussion of Pigou's 'theory of unemployment', and the argument is that Pigou falls squarely into the classical tradition and hence is subject to the criticisms which Keynes has already levelled against the classical theory of employment. He argues that if Pigou's sytem is to be determined, he requires the assumption that there is full employment equilibrium in the labour market; that is, that the volume of employment is determined by the intersection of the supply and demand curves for labour, and this presupposes that 'labour is always in a position to determine its own wage' (G.T., p.274).

Keynes's denial of this assumption, where wage means real wage, was, as we have argued in chapter 2, his major objection to the classical theory of employment. Pigou also admits that labour may stipulate for a given money-wage, and not for a given real wage, but does not realise that this requires a modification to his equational system, since it introduces another unknown. Hence in his discussion of Pigou's theory of unemployment (which is really somewhat of a misnomer) Keynes brings both objections which he earlier brought against the classical theory of the labour market.

Chapter 20 discusses the employment function, which is the inverse of the aggregate supply function, and which relates the quantity of effective demand to the corresponding volume of employment. Perhaps the most interesting section of the chapter is section III, where he applies his theory to the case where aggregate demand expands above the level of full employment. In this case, prices and wages will both rise in the same proportion as expenditure, with output remaining unchanged. Here the 'crude quantity theory of money' will hold; prices will be proportional to MV. In practice, though, certain qualifications ought to be borne in mind, particularly concerning the effects of inflation on income distribution. So the General Theory can be applied to booms as well as to recessions; it is perhaps wrong to write, as Hicks does, that 'the General Theory of Employment is the Economics of Depression' (see Hicks, 1937, p. 138).[2]

Chapter 21 discusses the theory of prices. This is fairly straightforward; once the money-wage is known and the volume of employment is determined, the real wage and hence the price level can be determined. In chapter 22, the theory is applied to the problem of the trade cycle. Keynes regards the trade cycle as mainly due to fluctuations in the marginal efficiency of capital, and suggests possible remedies. A 'crisis' may be caused by a collapse in the marginal efficiency of capital. Chapters 23 and 24 conclude the book.

In the section of the book discussed in this chapter, Keynes has been applying his theory, the construction of which by now is complete, to a number of problems, the most important of which is the effect of wage flexibility on output and employment and has reached various conclusions, which differ radically from those reached by the classical economists.

The most important challenge to Keynes has come in this area; it has been suggested that his analysis of the effects of money-wage reductions on output and employment is incomplete and that a sufficient reduction in money-wages and prices can always be relied upon to restore full employment. This argument is that based upon the Pigou effect, which concentrates on the effects of falling wages and prices on the propensity to consume.

There are two strands to the argument; the first is the argument that a fall in the price level will increase the personal sector's wealth. A necessary condition for the Pigou effect argument to work is that there should be in the economy an asset either with a fixed money price or the nominal value of which will not decline proportionately with a decline in the price level and which is regarded as constituting 'net wealth' for the private sector; that is, either it is not regarded as a liability as far as the private sector is concerned, or if it is, its valuation as a liability is less than its valuation as an asset. There has been controversy over the range of assets which satisfy this criterion. Money [3] is normally regarded as such an asset; government bonds are sometimes regarded as another of these assets; however, it has been argued against this position that government bonds are not net wealth, in that rational individuals should discount back to the present the tax payments which are required to service the interest payments on the bonds and consolidate this into their wealth. The case has been forcefully argued by Barro (1974). The issue is still controversial; some economists would tend to consider it ludicrous to attribute to individuals the degree of rationality ('hyperrationality') required if the argument is to go through. Many economists incorporate government bonds as constituents of net wealth in macro-economic models — see, for example, Blinder and Solow (1973) pp. 324-5. However, it is not necessary for us to enter into these arguments; as long as there exists one asset with the requisite properties, then the argument based on the Pigou effect can go through. The second strand of the argument is to suppose that the marginal propensity to consume out of wealth is positive and bounded away from zero. If this is so, then consumption can be raised to any desired level, and *a fortiori* to a level sufficient to restore full employment, if wealth can be increased sufficiently. But the first assumption ensures that this in fact can be done. By a sufficient deflation of the price level, wealth can be increased to any desired level and hence, it can always be used to restore full employment. This will be so even if deflation, by raising the real interest rate, reduces investment, provided that there is a lower bound to the level of investment; for the above argument entails that consumption can be raised sufficiently to outweigh any *finite* decrease in the level of investment.

Advocates of the Pigou effect stress that they are not recommending wage deflation as a policy measure. They concede that, in practice, the Pigou effect would be very slow in working, it being very difficult, if not impossible, to effect the requisite degree of wage and price deflation. They also concede that wage deflation may have undesirable side effects, which would be avoided if the Keynesian 'remedy' of monetary expansion were adopted. For example, there may be severe redistributional problems; there may be bankruptcies and because of these problems the initial reaction on the propensity to consume may be perverse. So wage deflation is not advocated as policy; what is suggested, however, is that it shows that on purely theoretical grounds the Keynesian contention that the possibility of an under-employment equilibrium does not rely on wage rigidity is invalid. For example, Johnson writes: 'the Pigou effect finally disposes of the Keynesian contention that under-employment equilibrium does not depend on the assumption of wage rigidity' (Johnson, 1964, p. 239).

Writers trying to defend Keynesian economics on the theoretical level have normally responded to this challenge by denying the relevance of the Pigou effect for some reason or other. These attempts have normally failed, after all, the argument based on the Pigou effect rests, as is argued above, on two fairly weak assumptions. Leijonhufvud, for example, has an argument against the Pigou effect which goes somewhat as follows: Keynes's diagnosis of the problem was that relative prices are wrong. A situation of unemployment occurs because the long-term rate of interest is too high and hence the demand price for capital goods is too low. What is required, he suggests, is not an overall deflation of the price level but a change in relative prices (see Leijonhufvud, 1967, p. 308; Leijonhufvud, 1968, pp. 328, 330). The argument seems to confuse necessary and sufficient conditions. A fall in the interest rate may be sufficient to restore full employment; it does not follow that it will be necessary; a fall in the absolute price level may also be sufficient to restore full employment and no argument has been given for supposing that this might not be the case.

The position taken here will be that the argument based on the Pigou effect is valid in showing that extreme wage flexibility will lead to full employment, but that this does not threaten Keynesian economics either practically or theoretically. In particular, the argument does not show that Keynesian economics was based on the 'special' assumption of money-wage rigidity. Suppose we scrutinize the argument in slightly more detail; the argument shows that with wage flexibility aggregate demand will rise towards the full employment level; the argument is based on the effects on the propensity to consume. But this shows that it is the

Keynesian theoretical apparatus which is being used to derive the conclusion; as we have seen Keynes considers that the volume of employment will only change if either the propensity to consume, the marginal efficiency of capital schedule, or the rate of interest are affected. So Keynes could have added the Pigou effect to his catalogue of the effects of wage flexibility on output and employment; he admits that his list of effects 'is not a complete catalogue of all the complex reactions of wage reductions in the complex real world. But [they] cover, I think, those which are usually the most important' (G.T., p. 264).

Since the argument based on the Pigou effect hence presupposes the Keynesian theoretical framework, it can hardly be used to undermine it.

If we regard the Keynesian claim as the claim that there can be under-employment equilibrium with perfectly flexible money-wages, then it must be conceded that the Pigou effect argument is decisive against that claim. However if we regard Keynes's achievement as the construction of a theoretical framework for analysing the behaviour of the economy when the labour market does not necessarily clear, then the argument does not undermine that theoretical framework; all it does do is to enable us to delimit the (extremely restrictive) conditions under which the system will continuously generate full employment. So the Pigou effect argument in no way threatens Keynesian economics; recognition of the Pigou effect is perhaps an omission by Keynes but in no way a serious one.

There seems to be no evidence in the General Theory that Keynes was aware of or discussed the Pigou effect at all; this is, for example, confirmed by Patinkin, who writes: 'There are several passages in the "General Theory" which reflect Keynes' implicit assumption that the real-balance effect does not directly influence the commodity market' (Patinkin, 1965, p. 634). However, there is some evidence that Keynes came close to acknowledging a real-balance effect. Take, for example, the following two passages: '... if the quantity of money is virtually fixed, it is evident that its quantity in terms of wage-units can be indefinitely increased by a sufficient reduction in money-wages' (G.T., p. 226) and 'if a man is enjoying a windfall increment in the value of his capital, it is natural that his motives towards current spending should be strengthened...' (G.T., p. 94). If Keynes had put these two ideas together, then it seems that he would have generated a real balance effect; however, there is no evidence that he did, and in his discussion of the effect of deflation on aggregate demand seems to concede only that higher real balances might work through lowering the rate of interest. As Leijonhufvud writes: '... there can be no doubt that Keynes meant that an increase in real balances, whether by injection or deflation, would have a significant effect on employment only by lowering the rate of interest and therefore affecting aggregate demand' (Leijonhufvud, 1968, pp. 323–4). However, we must take issue with Leijonhufvud when he writes: '... Keynes conceded that as a matter of logic, deflation could work' (Leijonhufvud, 1968, p. 324). But this is not something which Keynes does, in fact, concede. His conclusion is that the effect of deflation will under certain circumstances be equivalent to the effects of an expansionary monetary policy, and will therefore be subject to the same limitations in raising output. Deflation might well not work if the economy is in the liquidity trap or if investment is interest-insensitive.

Kuenne has argued that Keynes's divergence from classical theory consisted in his claim that he had constructed a theory in which an underemployment equilibrium is possible. He writes: 'Keynes' fundamental challenge to neoclassical theory is quite clear: it lies in his construction of a model in which flexibility of the money-wage rate cannot eliminate an excess supply of labour' (Kuenne, 1963, p. 347) and Keynes's theory is 'a system which yielded an excess supply of labour with no tendency toward self-correction' (Kuenne, 1963, p. 356). Both these passages are cited in Leijonhufvud (1968), pp. 316–7. If this is what Keynes's theory was then the argument based on the Pigou effect is clearly decisive in showing that the Keynesian claim is incorrect. However, it is argued here that this is not a correct interpretation of Keynes. Keynes certainly did not believe that he had constructed a system in which money-wage flexibility could not reduce or eliminate an excess supply of labour: 'A reduction in money-wages is quite capable in certain circumstances of affording a stimulus to output, as the classical theory supposes' (G.T., p. 247). He emphasizes that his difference from the classical theory is primarily one not of conclusion, but of analysis. Instead, our interpretation is that Keynes's achievement is his construction of an analytical framework whereby the level of involuntary unemployment can be determined. If we adopt this interpretation, then, as has already been argued, the Pigou effect is something which can be incorporated into the analysis; it is in no way destructive of Keynes's theoretical framework.

The view has sometimes been expressed that large persistent price movements of the type which are required if the Pigou effect is to operate are incompatible with the proper functioning of the monetary economy Keynes was considering. For example, Power writes: 'it is only in the reach of what might be called the pathology of monetary economy that the type of behaviour crucial to the operation of the wealth effect is relevant — that is, in situations of persistent inflation and deflation' (see Power, 1959, p. 142). Lerner is also cited in conjunction with this point of view, as is Keynes's chapter 17. However, there seems to be no evidence that Keynes actually made use of this point in his discussion of the effects of money-wage changes. For example, he suggests that there may be conditions when 'prices would be in unstable equilibrium when investment was at the crucial level, racing to zero whenever investment was below it, and to infinity whenever it was above it' (G.T., pp. 269-70). He suggests that large-scale price instability may have highly undesirable consequences: '[it may] make business calculations futile in an economic society functioning after the manner of that in which we live' (G.T., p. 269). But nowhere in this chapter is there the suggestion that a high degree of price instability is incompatible with a monetary economy or that his theory is inapplicable to this case. Chapter 17 is, as has already been argued, largely a speculative enquiry into the nature of a monetary economy and is not integrated into the rest of the theory.

The views taken in this chapter about the effects of wage-flexibility on output and employment are almost identical to those reached by Patinkin:

Clearly, Keynes recognized the importance of wage rigidities in the real world. Nevertheless ... these rigidities do not constitute a logically necessary part of his theory of unemployment.... Thus wage rigidities ... are not an assumption of the analysis, but the policy conclusion which Keynes reaches after investigating the results to be expected from wage flexibility (Patinkin, 1965, p. 643).

This concludes the discussion of the last two books of Keynes's General Theory. In the next chapter, the relationship of the

General Theory to some of his other works will be discussed, and in the final chapter, some conclusions will be drawn.

NOTES

1   This is computed as follows. Suppose inflation is expected to be p. Then £1 now will buy goods worth $£1/(1+p)$ a year hence and hence the return on money will be

$$1/(1+p)-1 = \frac{1-(1+p)}{(1+p)} = \frac{-p}{(1+p)}$$

which yields the figure given in the text when $p = -0 \cdot 10$ per cent. More generally a fixed price asset with a nominal return of r will have a real return of $(r-p)/(1+p)$; this is similar to the formula more normally given, $r-p$, when small rates of inflation (or deflation) are being considered but is more accurate when more severe inflations or deflations are being considered.

2   Keynes does, however, seem to assume that the labour market is in equilibrium in booms; he does not seem to contemplate the possibility that there might be excess demand for labour. Consideration of the latter possibility has led, for example, to the development of the concept of the supply multiplier (see Barro and Grossman, 1974).

3   Sometimes a distinction is made between 'outside' money (that issued by the government and 'inside' money (that which is a liability of the commercial banks). It is sometimes argued that only 'outside' money constitutes net wealth, so that the Pigou effect only works if there is 'outside' money in the economy. However, this distinction and its implications have been forcefully and convincingly criticized. On this, see Johnson (1969) and Patinkin (1969).

7 Keynes's *General Theory* and its Relationship to his Other Works

The main purpose of this book is to give an interpretation of Keynes's General Theory, and his other works have only been discussed inasmuch as they impinge upon this goal. The author feels that the procedure of concentrating on the General Theory can be justified, as it is that book which has had the major impact on post-war economic thought and which embodies the essence of what is now known as Keynesian economics. Nevertheless, an evaluation of the relationship of Keynes's General Theory to his other writings will hopefully be of some value; a discussion of Keynes's intellectual development, as evidenced in his writings, may well shed light on the General Theory, moreover, as Hicks writes (see Hicks, 1967, p. 189), there is much of permanent value in Keynes which was not absorbed into the General Theory where Keynes's concern is almost entirely with the problems of a closed economy; those who would like to read what he wrote on the problems of an open economy must look elsewhere.

In this chapter, the primary focus will be on the *Tract on Monetary Reform* (hereafter cited in references as T.M.R.) and on the *Treatise on Money* (hereafter cited in references as T.M.) In what follows, a brief description of these works will be given and an attempt will be made to trace the development of Keynes's thought on monetary matters and to identify some common and contrasting features in the three books.

The *Tract on Monetary Reform* is the earliest of the three works; it is also the shortest and most readable. In the first chapter, Keynes discusses the social consequences of price-level movements, either in the upwards direction (inflation) or in the downwards direction (deflation). He identifies two main effects; an effect on the distribution of wealth and another on the production of wealth. Inflation in particular is argued to be more likely to be adverse to investors whereas deflation is more likely to retard output and employment. The discussion of the effects of change in the value of money is in some respects remarkably up to date. For example he wrote that: 'When the value of money is greatly fluctuating, the distinction between capital and income becomes confused' (T.M.R., p. 29) and the distinction in question was one of the principal concerns of the recent Meade Committee's report on the direct taxation system (see Meade, 1978). The second chapter considers inflation as a form of taxation; again, there are foreshadowings of more recent discussion of the subject; in the third chapter, Keynes discusses the theoretical foundations of his treatment of price level changes; he employs a form of the quantity theory of money, of which he writes: 'This Theory is fundamental. Its correspondence with fact is not open to question' (T.M.R., p. 74). Nevertheless, only in the long run is a proportionate relationship between money and prices asserted; indeed, it is in this context that he makes his famous remark that 'in the long run we are all dead' (T.M.R., p. 80). In the shorter run, variations in velocity may preclude proportionality between money and prices; hence the task of the central bank in controlling and stabilizing the price level is made correspondingly harder. But, although Keynes does concede that changes in the money supply may not produce proportional movements in the price level in the short run, the basic theoretical apparatus he uses is that of the quantity theory; movements in the money supply are assumed to be the main factor behind price level movements and price level fluctuations are to be explained mainly in terms of fluctuations in the money supply. A discussion of purchasing power parity follows the discussion of the quantity theory of money, and there is a discussion of the foreign exchanges. The next chapter discusses the question of whether monetary policy should be directed towards stabilizing the value of money or towards maintaining a stable exchange rate. Keynes's conclusion is that 'the stability of prices, credit, and employment [is] of paramount importance' (T.M.R., p. 176) and his last chapter makes some suggestions for attaining this, as well as for stabilizing the foreign exchange rate. It is not intended here to give a comprehensive evaluation of the *Tract on Monetary Reform* and its contribution to economics, but rather to analyse its relationship to Keynes's other works. In this connection, we might make the following points.

Keynes does not have an explicit, articulated theory of employment or unemployment in the *Tract on Monetary Reform*. The quantity theory of money is used to explain movements in prices, and changes in employment are consequential upon these movements in prices. Keynes also fails to produce an explicit theory of employment in the *Treatise on Money*, and movements in unemployment are similarly analysed in an ad hoc fashion. However, in the *Treatise on Money* as shall be seen, the quantity theory of money takes a less central position and the discussion is organized around the so-called 'fundamental equations' which are little more than tautologies; they differ from the quantity theory in that they include neither the quantity of money nor the velocity of circulation, although they are described as versions of the quantity theory of money (see T.M., i, p. 138).

Keynes does not discuss the effects of inflation much in the General Theory, although there are some brief passages which suggest that his views on the matter are substantially unaltered; for example, he argues that one of the consequences of a highly unstable price level would be 'to make business calculations futile in an economic society functioning after the manner of that in which we live' (G.T., p. 269). There is somewhat more discussion of inflation in the *Treatise on Money*, where Keynes uses the analytical apparatus of the 'fundamental equations' to distinguish between different types of inflation and to examine the differential effects each has on society (see, for example, T.M., i, pp. 155-6). There is also an echo of Keynes's discussion in the *Tract on Monetary Reform* when he discusses he appropriate degree of stability (or instability) of money-wages in the General Theory, and concludes that a stable level of money-wages would be desirable (see G.T., p. 270) although here he does not prescribe that monetary policy be used to stabilize money-wages.

Another point to make is that the *Tract on Monetary Reform* is very much concerned with the problems of an open economy as was the *Treatise on Money*, whereas the General Theory is almost entirely concerned with the theory of a closed economy; in this context, it should perhaps be mentioned that the General Theory is much more concerned with theoretical questions than either of the other two works are. Both the *Tract on Monetary Reform* and the *Treatise on Money* have a theoretical section, but are largely concerned with applying the theoretical framework in a number of contexts; the General Theory is primarily concerned 'with difficult questions of theory' (G.T., p. v).

The *Treatise on Money* is a very different type of book to the *Tract on Monetary Reform*. It is, as its name seems to suggest, a thorough and ponderous work. It was written over a number of years in the 1920s with a view to consolidating Keynes's reputation as one of the leading economists of the day and was probably intended as the definitive work on the subject for some time to come. Nevertheless, Keynes was by no means fully satisfied with the book when he had finished it. In the introduction he writes:

The ideas with which I have finished up are widely different from those with which I began. The result is, I am afraid, that there is a good deal in this book which represents the process of getting rid of the ideas which I used to have and of finding my way to those which I now have. (T.M., i, p. vi).

So Keynes concedes that the book is in a somewhat unsatisfactory state, and it would not therefore be surprising if we find inconsistencies in the work. Reasons for the unsatisfactory state of the work probably include its long period of genesis, over which Keynes's thought was changing, and the fact that it was subject to little pre-publication discussion and criticism.

Nevertheless, the discussion of the *Treatise on Money* does seem to be organized around the so-called 'fundamental equations', and in what follows an attempt will be made to expound the basic theoretical apparatus of the *Treatise on Money*, as well as to identify aspects of the *Treatise on Money* which anticipate parts of the General Theory.

The 'fundamental equations' can be stated in a number of ways. Perhaps the simplest way is that given on p. 138 of the *Treatise on Money*:

$$P = W_1 + Q_1/R \qquad (7.1)$$
$$Z = W_1 + Q/O \qquad (7.2)$$

where P is the price level of consumption goods, Z is the price level of output as a whole (this is an appropriate index of the prices of the two types of goods in the economy, consumption-goods and investment-goods), Q_1 is the profit on the production and sale of consumption-goods, Q is the total profit in the economy, R is the output of consumption-goods, O is the total volume of output, and W_1 is the rate of earnings per unit of output (or the rate of efficiency earnings).

Keynes has chosen his units so that a unit of each good 'has the same cost of production on the base date' (T.M., i, p. 135) and hence feels justified in talking of the total volume of output, even though there are two distinct components of output. (The problems of aggregation and the measurement of total output or income concern Keynes as well in the General Theory, where he takes a slightly different approach.)

The 'fundamental equations', as written above, do not seem to embody particularly profound truths. The first one states that the price of a consumption-good is equal to the earnings of the factors of production used to produce it plus the per unit profits, and the second equation says the same for output as a whole.

These equations are intended by Keynes as tautologies or identities. Nevertheless, there seem to be a number of assumptions implicit in the construction of the equations. It seems to be assumed that there is no foreign trade (otherwise there would be a term for the price of imports) and that an appropriate index of output and of the general price level can be found. Keynes recognizes the tautological nature of his 'fundamental equations' but argues that 'Their only point is to analyse and arrange our material in what will turn out to be a useful way for tracing cause and effect, when we have vitalized them by the introduction of extraneous facts from the actual world' (T.M., i, p. 138).

In these equations profits are really what we would call 'supernormal profits' and are *excluded* from his definition of income.

So Keynes's national income accounting would go somewhat as follows:

$$R + I = O = R + S + Q \qquad (7.3)$$

and so

$$I - S = Q \qquad (7.4)$$

Therefore profits are equal to the difference between investment and savings, and, similarly, Q_1 is equal to $I' - S$, where I' is the cost of new investment (to be distinguished from I, its value).

So the 'fundamental equations' can be rewritten in the form:

$$P = W_1 + (I' - \underline{S})/R \qquad\qquad (7.5)$$

and

$$Z = W_1 + (I - \underline{S})/O \qquad\qquad (7.6)$$

In the *Treatise on Money*, Keynes in fact derived these equations before deriving equations (7.1) and (7.2). The procedure adopted here is perhaps more helpful, since equations (7.1) and (7.2) seem much more obvious than equations (7.5) and (7.6). Entrepreneurs' normal remuneration must be included in W_1, since only excess or abnormal profits are included in Q.

These equations are still identities. However, by introducing behavioural considerations, Keynes generates a theory of how the price level might move and of how output and employment might expand and contract. He contends that 'Savings and Investment [decisions] ... are taken by two different sets of people influenced by different sets of motives, each not paying very much attention to the other' (T.M., i, p. 279). He seems to take this to mean that the values of investment and savings are largely independent of each other; there is no link such as that postulated in the General Theory. Nowhere does Keynes seem to discuss the determinants of saving at any length, although he does write: 'the rate of saving ... is stimulated by a high rate of interest and discouraged by a low rate' (T.M., i, p. 154). Keynes here displays no such doubts as he later displays in the General Theory where he asserts that since the publication (in 1903!) of Cassel's *Nature and Necessity of Interest* 'it has been agreed ... that it is not certain that the sum saved out of a given income necessarily increases when the rate of interest is increased' (G.T., p. 182). Investment is argued to depend negatively on the interest rate, and the role of monetary policy is argued to be that of ensuring equilibrium in the economy, the condition for which is that investment equals saving. Excess profits, which arise when investment is greater than saving, lead entrepreneurs to try to expand output and employment; subnormal or negative excess profits lead them to try to contract output and employment, although the micro-economic basis for these assumptions about how entrepreneurs react to abnormal profits is by no means clear. In their attempt to expand output, entrepreneurs bid more eagerly for factors of production, and hence tend to raise their price;

similarly in a downturn, when excess profits are negative, there will be a tendency for factor prices to be forced down.

So by adding on assumptions about the components of the 'fundamental equations', Keynes is able to build a theory of cyclical fluctuations. As an illustration, he considers an economy which produces bananas, and examines the effects that a thrift campaign might have on the economy which is initially in balance in the sense that savings equal investment (see T.M.,i, pp. 176-8). The thrift campaign leads to a fall in the price of bananas, since, at least instantaneously, the supply of bananas is unchanged whereas the income devoted to purchase them is reduced (there seems to be a very close resemblance to the Marshallian short run here). In effect, there is a redistribution of income to consumers from producers; this means, however, that entrepreneurs are suffering abnormal losses and they react to this by curtailing production and reducing employment. This will continue until or unless investment and savings are brought to equality with one another. Thus, according to Keynes, the process will continue until either:

(a) all production ceases and the entire population starves to death; or (b) the thrift campaign is called off or peters out as a result of the growing poverty; or (c) investment is stimulated by some means or another so that its cost no longer lags behind the rate of saving (T.M.,i, p. 178).

Note that Keynes does not give the solution which a reading of the General Theory would suggest, namely that output and income fall and hence the volume of savings falls as well. Alternative (b) is perhaps closest to this, but presumably the thrift campaign's effect is to change the marginal propensity to consume (MPC); Keynes only considers a change in the MPC to its former level as a possible equilibrating mechanism; he does not consider the possibility that savings might change with an unchanged MPC because of a change in income. The following comments on the type of trade-cycle theory Keynes introduced in his *Treatise on Money* might be made.

First, Keynes carries over from the *Tract of Monetary Reform* his conception of the nature of the enterprise: 'The Fundamental Problem of Monetary Theory is ... to exhibit the causal process by which the price-level is determined, and the method of transition from one position of equilibrium to another' (T.M.,i,

p. 133). So the aim of the theory is to explain the determination of the price-level; the determination of the level of output and employment is not considered to be a problem to be solved. Keynes does consider movements of output and employment, although he does not have a rigorous theory of how they are determined. It is assumed that entrepreneurs try to expand or contract output depending upon whether profits are excessive or subnormal, but what determines the equilibrium level of output and the extent to which entrepreneurs expand or contract output is not discussed; movements in output and employment are analyzed in an ad hoc fashion. It is not true to say that the 'fundamental equations' are based on an assumption of constant output; they can be interpreted as holding when output changes, although care must be taken in applying them in such circumstances, for the rate of efficiency earnings (the rate of earnings per unit of output) may change with the level of output. However, much of the analysis based on the 'fundamental equations' does seem to involve either an implicit assumption of constant output or an assumption that changes in the level of output do not have some of the consequences they might otherwise have been expected to have. For example, Keynes discusses the 'Widow's Cruse' (T.M.,i, p.139) where an increase in entrepreneurs' propensity to spend leads to a corresponding increase in their profits. Subsequent writers have pointed out that this was based on an assumption of constant output.

More seriously, the effect of changes in output and income on savings is not considered, and this makes a crucial difference to the analysis. For example, in the banana economy, equilibrium could have been restored quite simply by a fall in output. We are given the impression in the *Treatise on Money* that whenever a discrepancy between investment and savings arises, then a long-drawn-out period of disequilibrium may occur, particularly if the change is in a downward direction, and it may only be the banking system which, by changing the rate of interest, can restore equilibrium. Instead, if output is allowed to change and the effect of income changes on savings is considered, then equilibrium can be quickly re-established by a fall in output.

So perhaps we can come to the following conclusions about the relationship between the three books. In the *Tract on Monetary Reform* and the *Treatise on Money* the theoretical apparatus used is one appropriate for determining the level of prices. Movements in output and employment are considered, but the theoretical treatment of these is somewhat ad hoc. Keynes notes in the introduction to the *General Theory* that the outstanding fault in the *Treatise on Money* was his failure to deal adequately with the effects of changes in output. We might add that he failed to have any adequate theory of the determination of the level of output, either in equilibrium or in disequilibrium. In the *General Theory*, the nature of the enterprise is seen quite differently; it is to construct a theory which enables the level of output and employment to be determined. The theory of the price level is somewhat relegated in importance, and it is only discussed at a relatively late stage in the book; it is, however, added on to the rest of the theory in a theoretically rigorous fashion. (With the money-wage exogenous, the theory enables the level of output to be determined. The marginal product of labour can then be determined, and this is assumed to be equal to the real wage. With the money-wage already determined, the price level is therefore determined. This is discussed in the General Theory, chapter 19.)

Hence we can see why Keynes regarded the development of the consumption function as so important in the development of his own thinking — see, for example, Keynes's letter quoted in Patinkin (1978), p. 66. It meant that as output changed, consumption and savings changed in the same direction, and hence a rise in investment could lead, via the multiplier, to a corresponding increase in savings; there would be no need for a long-drawn-out period of disequilibrium. Keynes's remark that he developed the theory of liquidity preference only after developing the consumption function may seem at first to be somewhat puzzling; after all, the elements of the speculative demand for money, with its emphasis on expectations, are present in the *Treatise on Money* (this shall be argued at greater length below). However, as has been argued elsewhere in this book, the theory of liquidity preference owes its importance to the type of disequilibrium system Keynes was constructing. With the development of the theory of effective demand and the consumption function, Keynes could mount an effective attack on the classical theory of the rate of interest. With this rejected, attention was focussed on the rate of interest in the demand for money equation, and this led to the development of the theory of liquidity preference. Hence although the elements of the theory might have been present in Keynes's work much earlier, only after the development of the theory of effective demand could it be seen how the theory of liquidity preference 'fitted in' to the overall theory. Many of the elements of the General Theory are present in the *Treatise on Money*, and to a discussion of some of the common elements — as well as of some of the differences — we now proceed.

The quantity theory of money is mentioned in both books, but in neither does it attain the importance attained in the *Tract on Monetary Reform* (the form of quantity theory employed there has already been discussed in this chapter) where it constitutes the theoretical framework of the book. In the *Treatise on Money*, as we have seen, the role of the quantity theory of money is much less central, and the theoretical core of the book centres around the 'fundamental equations' which, despite Keynes's statement to the contrary, are not forms of the quantity theory of money. Money and monetary policy enter in primarily through their effect on investment and also perhaps on savings (via the interest rate) and in this respect, the *Treatise on Money* is much more similar to the General Theory than to the *Tract on Monetary Reform*.

Nevertheless, in both the *Treatise on Money* and in the General Theory Keynes gives conditions under which his theory will generate a quantity theory of money. In the *Treatise on Money*, pages 146-7, Keynes concedes that in equilibrium — which here is a demanding condition — a crude form of the quantity theory of money is valid in the sense that an increase in the quantity of money will entail a corresponding increase in the price level. But he gives reasons for preferring his 'fundamental equations' to the form of the quantity theory he used in the *Tract on Monetary Reform*: 'they do lead up to what are generally our real *quaesita* ... whereas the alternative methods lead up, as we shall see, to various hotch-potch price-levels which are of no great interest in themselves' (T.M., i, p.221). So the price-level which features in the 'fundamental equations' is the price-level of output as a whole, which is what Keynes wants to focus on; whereas the price-level which features in the quantity equations of the *Tract on Monetary Reform* is the price-level appropriate for the multiplicity of purposes for which cash-balances are used; and this may be very different from the appropriate index for the price-level of output as a whole. Keynes's main reason, then, for rejecting the quantity theory framework as the theoretical core of his analysis concerns a point about the appropriate price-index to use.

It is somewhat different in the General Theory; the quantity theory of money is only mentioned towards the end of the book. Keynes's conception of the nature of the enterprise is fundamentally different. It is to examine 'the pure theory of what determines the actual employment of the available resources' G.T., p.4) and in developing his theory Keynes seems hardly to mention the quantity theory of money. Only when he has developed his theory of how the price-level is determined does he discuss the relationship of his theory to the quantity theory; he gives a number of simplifying assumptions under which his theory will generate a quantity theory of money (G.T., pp.295-6), but then does stress the simplifying nature of the assumptions.

The next topic to be discussed is that of the theory of the demand for money. In the *Tract on Monetary Reform*, Keynes's analysis of the demand for money seems to be very much in the quantity theory tradition: '. . . The *number* of notes which the public ordinarily have on hand is determined by the amount of *purchasing power* which it suits them to hold, or to carry about, and by nothing else' (T.M.R., p.76). This, in turn, is argued to depend on factors such as wealth and habits, which change rather slowly over time. Hence the demand for money function seems to be fairly stable, and is not subject to rapid or unpredictable shifts. The situation is different in the *Treatise on Money*. Here we seem to have the elements of Keynes's speculative demand for money. The terminology is somewhat different; the saver is assumed to decide upon the portion of his wealth which he will hold in the form of savings-deposits and the remainder is held in the form of securities. But the factors which affect this choice are basically those factors which influence the choice between money and bonds in the General Theory. (Perhaps we should remember that in the General Theory money is assumed to be co-extensive with bank deposits — see G.T., p.167, fn 1 — as is also the case in the T.M.) When discussing an individual who has become more disposed to hold his wealth in the form of savings-deposits, he writes:

his distaste for other securities is not absolute and depends on his expectations of the future return to be obtained from savings-deposits and from other securities respectively, which is obviously affected by the price of the latter — and also by the rate of interest allowed on the former. If, therefore, the price-level of other securities falls sufficiently, he can be tempted back into them (T.M., i, p.142).

Although there are a few differences of detail, this seems to be the essence of the speculative theory of the demand for money. This is acknowledged by Keynes in the General Theory in his footnote on p.169, although slightly later (pp.173-4), he argues that there are some divergences between his treatment of the matter in the *Treatise on Money* and that in the General Theory. However, we may certainly contend that the essence of Keynes's theory is contained in the *Treatise on Money*; and the distinction he makes between income-deposits, business-deposits and savings-deposits is closely related to the distinction made in the General Theory between the income-motive, the precautionary-motive and the speculative-motive. Nevertheless, we might treat the discussion of the demand for money in the General Theory as an improvement over that in the *Treatise on Money* in two senses. First, Keynes does, as we have seen, confess to some divergences in his treatment of the demand for money in the *Treatise on Money* from that in the General Theory; secondly, Keynes has perhaps integrated the theory of the demand for money more satisfactorily into the structure of his theory.

Investment is the next topic to be considered here. The theory of investment is hardly discussed at all in the *Tract on Monetary Reform*, although the distinction between the real and the money interest rate, and its significance for investment, is discussed. Investment is discussed more fully in the *Treatise on Money*; Keynes gives a fairly clear account (T.M., pp.201-3) of investment and the effect of interest rate changes on investment. What is important, Keynes suggests, is the relationship between the demand price of capital goods and their cost of production. The demand price of capital goods, in turn, depends upon two things — 'on the estimated net prospective yield from fixed capital ... and on the rate of interest at which this future yield is capitalised' (T.M., i, p.202). And although changes in the rate of interest are unlikely to affect the first factor, they are definitely likely to affect the second factor, the rate of discount of future returns. (Keynes's discussion is in fact slightly more sophisticated and involves the distinction between the bond rate of interest and bank rate.) Keynes seems to be in no doubt that changes in the interest rate will change the demand price for new capital goods, and argues that the actual change in demand might be 'greater than one might expect if one was to concentrate all one's attention on the mere change of [say] 2½ to 5 per cent in the value of such goods due to the change in the rate of interest' (T.M., i, p. 203) because of the possibility of accelerating or postponing investment plans. So it seems that the essence of Keynes's theory of investment as expounded in the General Theory is already in the *Treatise on Money*; the level of investment is determined by the interaction of supply and demand in the capital-goods industry and the factors which influence the demand for capital goods are basically the same in the two books; however, there are some differences. The concept of the marginal efficiency of capital is one which is introduced in the General Theory; as has been remarked on before (see Patinkin, 1976, p. 13) there seems to be a complete lack of marginal analysis in the *Treatise on Money*; concepts such as the marginal productivity of labour and the marginal efficiency of capital which are so prominent in the General Theory, do not appear at all in the *Treatise on Money*. Also, although Keynes does recognize that investment will depend on expectations of what is to happen in the future and hence that uncertainty is relevant, this is not something which he stresses.

Not only does Keynes not mention the marginal productivity of labour, there seems to be virtually no analysis of the labour market at all in the *Treatise on Money*; again, this is something the *Treatise on Money* shares with the *Tract on Monetary Reform* but not with the General Theory. However, Keynes does discuss the possibility of 'spontaneous' changes in earnings, and devotes a section of one of his chapters to discussing it (T.M., i, pp. 166-70). Trade unions may be one of the factors responsible for this, and they may also be responsible for imparting a degree of downward rigidity to the money-wage: 'Trade Unions in the old country present great obstacles to a reduction of money-wages' (T.M., i, p. 347). Here, again, there are certain resemblances to parts of the General Theory.

The 'paradox of thrift', as it is now known, is not discussed in the *Treatise on Money*, but it is recognized that changes in savings ratios may have apparently paradoxical conclusions, and in particular that it may not lead to an increase in the community's net wealth. According to the *Treatise on Money* model, an increase in savings which is not matched by a corresponding increase in investment will lead to a fall in the price of consumption-goods; this leads to a transfer of consumption from the savers to the consumers (Keynes does not consider the possibility that savers might modify their behaviour as the price level falls) and to a transfer of wealth to the savers from the producers, with total consumption and total wealth remaining unchanged (T.M., i, p. 174). Keynes does not consider the possibility that the change in the price-level might have wealth-effects. However, if investment rises with savings, then the net wealth of the community will increase. He writes: 'An act of saving by an individual may result either in increased investment or in increased consumption by the individuals who make up the rest of the community. The performance of the act of saving is in itself no guarantee that the stock of capital goods will be correspondingly increased' (T.M., i, p. 175).

This concludes the discussion of areas which the *Tract on Monetary Reform*, the *Treatise on Money* and the General Theory have in common. In conclusion, we might say that there are similarities between both the *Tract on Monetary Reform* and the *Treatise on Money* and between the *Treatise on Money* and the General Theory. In the first two works the nature of the enterprise is regarded as that of explaining the movement of prices, and changes in output are explained in an ad hoc fashion. In the *Tract on Monetary Reform* the quantity theory of money is central; it is less central in the *Treatise on Money* and has almost disappeared in the General Theory.

Many of the elements of the General Theory are already in the *Treatise on Money*; however, they are not integrated to form a theoretically coherent whole. We may add to Keynes's statement that 'the outstanding fault of the theoretical parts of that work ... [was] ... that I failed to deal thoroughly with the effects of *changes* in the level of output' (G.T. p. vii) the statement that he has also failed to explain or even to try to explain, how the level of output itself was determined. But this deficiency is definitely remedied in the General Theory.

8 Conclusion

Many diverse features have figured in previous interpretations of the General Theory. Factors such as money illusion, money-wage rigidity, the consumption function, liquidity preference, the liquidity trap, uncertainty, the role of money in the economy and a denial of Say's Law have all been mentioned as important or crucial factors in Keynes's theory and in the explanation of how it diverged from the classical theory. The main claim of the interpretation of the General Theory presented here is that it enables the role of *all* of these factors to be understood, related to each other and incorporated into a comprehensive interpretation of the book. The author is unaware of any other interpretation which does this successfully, and it is hoped that this interpretation will stand or fall by its success or failure in providing a plausible account of how these features fit into Keynesian theory. Hence in this concluding chapter the interpretation presented here will be summarized, and in presenting the summary an attempt will be made to explain how it is felt that each of the elements mentioned above fits into the theory.

PART I

In chapter 1 we gave an equational representation of the classical theory, or at least the theoretical framework underlying the classical theory. Here it might be appropriate to give an equational representation of the Keynesian system:

$$N^D = N^D(\underline{w/p}) \qquad (8.1)$$
$$N^S = N^S(\underline{w/p}) \qquad (8.2)$$
$$N = \min(N^D, N^S) \qquad (8.3a)$$
$$w = \bar{w} \qquad (8.3b)$$
$$Y = f(N) \qquad (8.4)$$
$$C(Y, i) + I(i) = Y \qquad (8.5)$$
$$\underline{m/p} = g(Y, i) \qquad (8.6)$$

where the notation used is the same as that used in the first chapter. This is a fairly standard representation of the Keynesian system, and does not pretend to be novel. Nor does it pretend to be unique. The problem to which this book is largely addressed is that of relating all the features of Keynesian economics mentioned in the opening paragraph of this chapter to the Keynesian system as represented by such a set of equations. In doing this, a three-fold distinction might be helpful. First, there are the arguments Keynes uses against the classical theory; in particular, the arguments against making the labour market clearing assumption and against Say's Law. Secondly, there are the arguments he uses and the considerations he adduces in constructing his own theory. Although Keynes's theory and the classical theory are, in their equational representation, rather similar (differing only in their third equation), the interpretation of some of the constituent equations does, because of the modifications made, change. And thirdly, there are the uses to which he puts his theory; for example, examining the conditions under which wage flexibility will ensure full employment.

In applying the theory, a discussion of the particular form the constituent functions are likely to have is often relevant, as is discussion of their stability. But such arguments, although useful when applying the theory, are in no way crucial to the theory and the way in which it differs from the classical theory.

In the paragraphs which follow, an attempt will be made to show how each of the factors mentioned earlier can be incorporated into a comprehensive picture of Keynesian economics:

1　Money illusion has a very limited role in the General Theory. It is given as a reason for doubting the classical theory of employment; this is perhaps just as well, as his argument against the classical theory solely on this score is incorrect. Money illusion might also lead to money-wage rigidity. By 'money-illusion' is meant a situation where absolute prices, such as the price level and the money-wage, independent of relative prices or real balances, enter as arguments into agents' behaviour functions. Such behaviour may seem, strictly speaking, to be irrational; however Keynes suggests that an aggregate labour supply function exhibiting apparent money illusion may be produced by a system of highly structured wage differentials which is maintained by individuals' utility functions having other individuals' wage levels, as well as their own, as arguments. Thirdly, some other parts of the theory may be characterized by money illusion. For example, Patinkin (see Patinkin, 1965, pp. 637-42) has accused him of assuming money illusion in the speculative demand for money function. This is certainly justified if Keynes is interpreted as making the *nominal* speculative demand for money dependent solely upon the interest rate; and this is a very plausible interpretation, as Patinkin argues. However, this deficiency can be remedied without too much difficulty, and the theory can be repaired at little cost. So, in Keynes's theory, money illusion is primarily relevant as a reason for doubting the classical theory of employment; it can also be used to explain the amount of wage rigidity actually exhibited in the economy.

2 As emphasized before in this book, Keynes did not assume money-wage rigidity. His criticism of the classical theory of employment contained in chapter 2, was not that the theory was invalid because money-wages were rigid. (This seems to be the textbook interpretation.) His first criticism is that the theory is invalid, or at least indeterminate, if there is money illusion in the labour supply function; his second, and major criticism is that the labour market may not be stable, and hence the assumption that it clears it not justified, at least at the outset. In constructing his theory, Keynes assumes an exogenous or parametric money-wage and, having constructed his theory, he can consider the effect on output and employment of changing the money-wage. Nowhere, then, does Keynes assume money-wage rigidity; he may well have believed that the money-wage was characterized by a large amount of rigidity and perhaps the argument based on money illusion may, at least partially, account for this. It is also necessary that the theory should be applicable to the case where money-wages are in fact rigid. For example, in discussing Pigou's 'theory

of unemployment', he writes: 'A theory cannot claim to be a general theory, unless it is applicable to the case where ... money-wages are fixed, just as much as to any other case' (G.T., p. 276). It is also true that, following his discussion of the effects of wage flexibility on output and employment, he concludes that the most desirable policy would be one of wage rigidity. So Keynes may have believed in wage rigidity and have constructed a theory capable of application to the case where money-wages are rigid, but he certainly did not *assume* that money-wages are rigid. The arguments designed to show that Keynes either assumed or ought to have assumed money-wage rigidity are also not successful. Alternative reasons can be given for the persistent failure of a market to clear, and the argument based on the Pigou effect does not show that Keynes ought to have assumed money-wage rigidity or that his theory is in some sense a 'special case' of the classical theory.

3   The consumption function, with income as an argument, is often stated to be a major, in fact sometimes the major, innovation of the General Theory. Clower has provided us with a reason for thinking that when the labour market does not clear, quantities — and hence income — will enter into the market demand functions. Hence it is plausible that in the disequilibrium context of Keynes's theory, he should come up with the type of consumption function he did come up with. The suggestion is not that Keynes had the type of theory presented by Clower explicitly in mind when writing the General Theory, but that Clower's analysis makes it plausible that Keynes should have hit upon the consumption function when constructing his theory. Keynes also assumed that the marginal propensity to consume was between zero and unity, and he called this a 'very obvious conclusion'. However, Clower's analysis in no way justifies this particular conclusion; it is quite possible to give examples of cases where the marginal propensity to consume is negative. One example would be where leisure and consumption are highly complementary; the relaxation of a current constraint on labour supply may lead to less current consumption; instead, all the extra income will go to finance increased consumption and leisure in the future. But given the consumption function an assumption of an MPC between zero and unity would seem to be a very obvious assumption to make, perhaps akin to the assumption that demand curves are downward

sloping. In both cases, further analysis is required to make precise the conditions under which the 'obvious' conclusion will in fact hold.

4 The theory of liquidity preference arose out of Keynes's critique of the classical theory of the interest rate. With the relaxation of the labour market clearing assumption, it was no longer possible to determine the interest rate without using the money market equilibrium condition (equation (8.6)). Hence it became necessary to use the whole simultaneous equational framework in order to determine the interest rate; in particular, it became necessary to consider the effect of the interest rate on the demand for money. It would perhaps be wrong to say that the classical economists completely ignored the effect of the interest rate on the demand for money; counter-examples can and have been given (see Patinkin, 1965, pp. 630-3). But since the interest rate for them was already determined elsewhere, they could subsume the effect of the rate of interest on the demand for money within the functional form of the demand for money function itself, and hence they did not tend to emphasize the role of interest in the demand for money function. With Keynes, it is different; the form of the demand for money function will be of crucial importance in explaining how changes in the exogenous variables of the model affect the endogenous variables. The impression is sometimes given that Keynes realised that the demand for money depends upon the interest rate and the classical economists had not realised this. But this is misleading; the reason Keynes stressed the role of interest in the demand function for money is that the structure of his theory required an appraisal of the relevance of the interest rate as an argument of the demand for money function, whereas this was not necessary for the classical economists.

5 In order to justify a dependence of the demand for money on the interest rate, Keynes uses arguments based on uncertainty; he includes the argument normally given for the speculative demand for money. The main role of uncertainty in Keynes's theory is to underpin the speculative demand for money; it is also argued that the marginal efficiency of capital schedule might be highly unstable because of the precariousness of expectations about the future. However, as argued earlier, this is not a part of Keynes's theory which is in any respect crucial inasmuch as his divergence from the classics is concerned. It is relevant when applying the

theory to a number of economic problems, but not in actually constructing the theory. So uncertainty does play an important role in the structure of Keynes's theory, but perhaps a far less important role than is sometimes attributed to it by some writers.

6   The concept of the liquidity trap has also featured prominently in discussions of Keynesian economics. As discussed in the text, Keynes's views on the matter are complex, but perhaps can be summed up as follows: there are reasons for thinking that the rate of interest will tend to be sticky about its current level, but this will not prevent a sufficiently determined monetary policy from reducing interest rates. However, there is also likely to be a floor to the interest rate for a number of reasons, and this may well prove a barrier to an expansionary monetary policy. But these are conjectures about the specific form of the demand for money function, and hence do not relate in any essential way to Keynes's divergence from the classical theory. What is important in Keynes is the dependence of the demand for money on the interest rate, and the role of uncertainty in underpinning this dependence.

7   The question of the role of money in Keynes's theory is slightly more problematical. It is undoubtedly true that Keynes regarded the problems he was dealing with as problems peculiar to a monetary economy. For example, in his introduction, he writes: 'A monetary economy, we shall find, is essentially one in which changing views about the future are capable of influencing the quantity of employment and not merely its direction' (G.T., p. vii). Slightly later, he writes: 'We shall discover, however, that Money plays an essential part in our theory of the Rate of Interest; and we shall attempt to disentangle the peculiar characteristics of Money which distinguish it from other things' (G.T ., p. 32). As has already been argued, money plays an important role in the General Theory in the theory of the determination of the interest rate; money is not neutral; changes in the money supply will affect output and employment through their effect on the interest rate. This contrasts with money's role in the classical theory, where changes in the money supply affect just prices and money-wages, leaving all real variables unchanged. This is so even if the interest rate enters into the demand for money function. It is a consequence of Keynes's construction of a model in which the labour market need not clear that money has this more important

role in the economy; hence Keynes's stress on the importance of monetary policy in the economy, a stress which would not be consistent with an espousal of the classical position. (It might be argued that the classical economists did recognize that monetary expansion might affect real variables in the short run. But this result in no way seems to follow from any theoretical structure of theirs). So money has a more important role to play in Keynes's theoretical schema than it did in the classical theory. Keynes also had some speculative thoughts to offer about the nature of money and a monetary economy. His conclusion is that money is important both because it is a non-reproducible store of value and also because of its liquidity properties (though this is an inadequate summary). The suggestion is that in an economy without an asset with these properties, aggregate demand will always stay at or around its full employment level; so only in a monetary economy can 'changing views about the future' have an effect on the quantity of employment.

8 The concepts of aggregate demand and supply and the associated concept of effective demand figure heavily in Keynesian economics. They were introduced by Keynes in order to determine the level of output and employment in the economy, after he had concluded that the classical arguments for the stability of full employment equilibrium were invalid, and therefore it became necessary to construct a new framework in order to determine output and employment. So the concepts of aggregate demand and aggregate supply became important for analyzing the type of problem Keynes was concerned with, but were not particularly relevant for the classical theorists. Hence Keynes's complaint about the disappearance of the concept of effective demand from the writings of the clasical economists (see G.T., p. 32); for given the assumption of full employment equilibrium, the concept becomes redundant; only in the type of disequilibrium situation with which Keynes is concerned do the aggregate demand and supply curves regain their utility. So again, the emphasis on aggregate demand and supply is a consequence of the disequilibrium structure of Keynes's theory.

9 The final topic to be integrated into the picture of how the various elements mentioned in the introduction fit into the interpretation put forward here, is Say's Law. As was emphasized in earlier discussion, it should be clearly distinguished from

Walras' Law. The interpretation presented here is that it provides foundations to classical economics alternative to those provided by the full employment equilibrium assumption. It is an argument which concentrates on the output market rather than on the labour market, but which can be used to argue for the same conclusion, since the two markets are connected by a production function. Keynes has various arguments against Say's Law; he suggests that it is based on highly restrictive assumptions which we have no reason to believe should hold; he produces his alternative framework and within this framework, he argues, there is no need for output to be at the full employment level.

Perhaps it would be helpful to relate these points more explicitly to the distinction made earlier. The arguments concerning money illusion and Say's Law relate to Keynes's arguments against the classical theory. The consumption function, money, the theory of liquidity preference, uncertainty (inasmuch as it lies behind the liquidity preference schedule) and the aggregate demand and supply curves all relate to the way in which Keynes's theory differs from that of the classics. The liquidity trap and uncertainty (inasmuch as it implies an unstable MEC schedule) relate to the actual forms of the functions involved in the theory and are hence not theoretically crucial. Wage rigidity, since it was not assumed by Keynes, does not figure in the above classification. (Perhaps money should also be included in the first category as well when consideration is given to chapter 17 in the General Theory.

This concludes the summary of the interpretation of Keynes's General Theory presented in this book; the next question to be discussed is that of how the interpretation given here differs from those which have been given previously.

PART II

Hick's interpretation, expounded in his article 'Mr Keynes and the Classics' (Hicks, 1937) has been influential and will be discussed here. Our position will be that Hick's IS/LM framework is a possible schematization of the theory Keynes expounds in his book, but that Hicks is wrong in the principal innovations he attributes to Keynes, largely because he misrepresents classical theory.

Hicks's IS/LM framework is one of three diagrammatic techniques developed for expounding Keynes's theory. The first, and simplest, is the 'Keynesian-cross' diagram, as shown in Fig. 8.1.

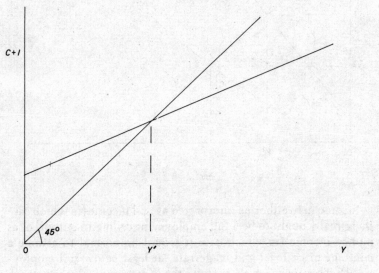

FIGURE 8.1

This diagram tells us that the equilibrium level of income will be where the aggregate supply of output is equal to the aggregate demand for output, which depends solely on the level of income. Keynes seemed to use a model of this type in the latter part of chapter 10, when he had developed the theory of effective demand and of the multiplier, but had not yet developed his theory of the interest rate. The theory is extremely crude, inasmuch as it considers neither the price level, the wage rate nor the interest rate as arguments of any of the constituent functions of the framework. This diagram is perhaps an expression of pure 'hydraulic' Keynesianism, to use Coddington's terminology (see Coddington, 1976, pp. 1263-7).

The IS/LM framework introduces the interest rate into the analysis, and it is depicted in Fig. 8.2.

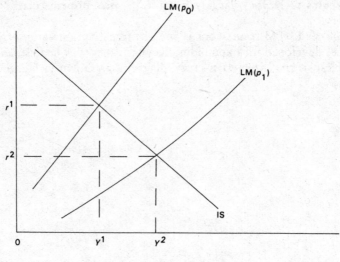

FIGURE 8.2

Income may either be interpreted as real income (in which case there really ought to be a full employment ceiling to output) or as money income (in which case it would be normal to assume a constant price level and wage rate, at least below full employment). This approach shares with the 'Keynesian-cross' approach the tendency to neglect aggregate supply considerations; it is assumed that the quantity of output demanded is supplied at the constant real wage. Equilibrium is determined at the point at which the IS curve, representing the combinations of r and Y which are consistent with equilibrium in the goods market, intersects the LM curve, which represents the combination of r and Y which are consistent with equilibrium in the money market. The third, and most sophisticated diagrammatic representation of the Keynesian system is that embodied in the so-called 'aggregate demand' and 'aggregage supply' framework; this should not be confused with Keynes's use of these terms. This enables the real wage to vary — as it should, if we assume diminishing returns — with the level of output. The aggregate demand curve is derived by making the LM curve in Fig. 8.2 a locus of points showing those combinations of income and the interest rate at which the real money supply is equal to real money demand. Hence the LM curve can be drawn for a given price level, but will shift with a change in the price level. Hence each price level will be associated with a certain level of real income; the locus of equilibrium combinations of price and income, in price-income space, may be designated the aggregate demand curve. The aggregate supply curve shows, for a given money-wage rate, the price level which will be associated with any level of output. Under competitive conditions, each level of output will be associated with a certain real wage; hence given the money-wage, the price level is determined. A pair of aggregate demand and supply curves is depicted in Fig. 8.3.

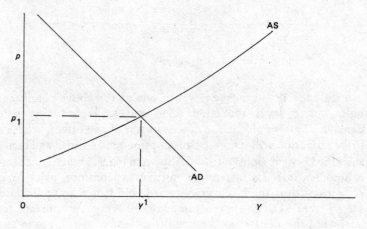

FIGURE 8.3

As the money-wage rate is parametric in the construction of the AS curve, the diagram is perhaps particularly appropriate for analyzing the effects of money wage reductions on output and employment. Money-wage reductions will shift the AS curve downwards as is shown in Fig. 8.4. Therefore it is both necessary and sufficient for money-wage reductions to increase output and employment that the AD curve is not vertical. Conditions under which the AD curve will be vertical can be defined: if the IS curve does not shift with the price level, then either the LM curve must be horizontal or the IS curve vertical (that is, there is a liquidity trap or expenditure is interest-insensitive). If price level changes

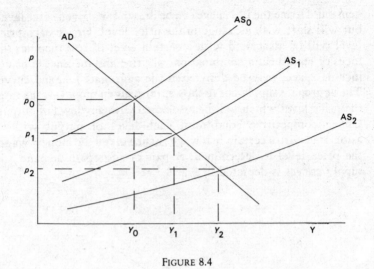

FIGURE 8.4

can shift the IS curve, then even if one of the above conditions holds, price level reductions can lead to higher aggregate demand. This would be the case with the Pigou effect, where a price reduction will increase consumption expenditure and hence shift the IS curve rightward, as is shown in Fig. 8.5 where with *both* a liquidity trap *and* interest-insensitive expenditure, price level reductions shift the IS curve outward, and hence boost income. Hence the AD/AS curve framework is very appropriate for analyzing the debate on the conditions under which wage and price reductions can lead to higher output and employment.

These diagrams illustrate different ways in which Keynes's theoretical apparatus might be illustrated. Keynes himself, on being asked to comment on Hicks's article mentioned earlier, replied that he had 'next to nothing to say by way of criticism' (Hicks, 1973, p.9); our position will be that IS/LM analysis, as an example of the three diagrammatic analyses we have depicted, is an appropriate representation of Keynes's theoretical framework.

Various objections to this point of view have, however, been raised. Davidson writes that IS/LM 'has the disadvantage of being based on a Walrasian general equilibrium approach' (see Davidson, 1978, p.175). This seems to be based on a misconception. According to the Walrasian general equilibrium approach,

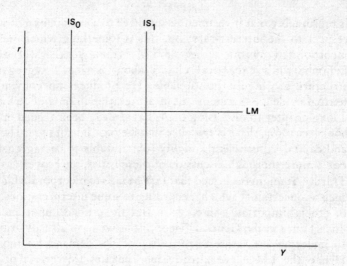

FIGURE 8.5

the auctioneer ensures that all markets clear, whereas in IS/LM, the labour market in general will not clear. It is true that the IS/LM model embodies an equilibrium concept, but then the concept of equilibrium is a very fundamental economic concept, and economic reasoning would be hard put to dispense with it. Leijonhufvud has also criticized the IS/LM framework as an appropriate vehicle for conveying Keynes's ideas, but it is not clear what his criticism; amount to. His arguments seem to concentrate on showing that Keynes did not assume or argue that the curves had special shapes (for example, that the demand for money becomes infinitely elastic at some interest rate or that investment is interest-inelastic) but this is not to be construed as an attack on the IS/LM framework itself, but on the attribution of specific values to some of the parameters underlying the model — this is argued in more detail in Jackman (1974). Leijonhufvud has also presented arguments concerning the aggregative structure of Keynes's model; he argues that in the General Theory, bonds and capital assets are aggregated. This claim, if it were correct, would not, however, undermine the claim that IS/LM is an appropriate representation of Keynes's theoretical framework; for one of the implications of bonds and capital assets being highly substitutable is presumably that investment is sensitive to a certain extent with respect to the interest-rate; but this is something which can be incorporated within the IS/LM framework. Moreover, Leijonhufvud's exegetical claims about Keynes's aggregative structure are highly questionable. He produces no convincing textual evidence to support his interpretation in spite of devoting a long chapter to discussing it. As has already been argued in this book (see p. 69), there is evidence that Keynes did not regard bonds and capital as sufficiently highly substitutable to be aggregated. For a more thorough discussion of these issues, see Froyen (1976). Thirdly, it might be argued that IS/LM fails to incorporate factors such as uncertainty which, according to some interpretations, are of crucial importance in Keynes. But the crucial importance of uncertainty in the General Theory is, as we have already argued, to underpin the interest-sensitivity of the demand for money. Hence the LM curve already incorporates this effect of uncertainty; uncertainty is therefore implicit in the IS/LM framework. The other consequence of uncertainty in the General Theory, a highly unstable and volatile investment schedule, can also be represented in IS/LM analysis; it leads to a highly unstable IS curve.

Hence IS/LM has not been shown to be an inadequate representation of Keynes's theoretical structure. However, we do have reason to dispute Hicks's conclusions regarding Keynes's divergence from classical economics, which centre on the role of interest in the demand for money function and the liquidity trap. This arises from the particular way he represents the classical theory; it will be argued here that this depiction is incorrect.

Hicks regards the classical theory as being composed essentially of the following equations:

$$M = KI \qquad \text{(M is money, I money income)} \qquad (8.7)$$
$$I_x = C(i) \qquad \text{(investment is a function of} \atop \text{the interest rate)} \qquad (8.8)$$
$$I_x = S(i, I) \qquad \text{(investment equals savings which} \atop \text{is a function both of the interest} \atop \text{rate and of the level of income)} \qquad (8.9)$$

Hicks, in considering how Keynes's theory differs from the above, introduces the rate of interest into equation (8.7), making the demand for money a function of the interest rate as well as of the level of income, and in this way draws his conclusion about the importance of liquidity preference in Keynes's theory.

But this framework differs markedly from that introduced as classical theory in chapter 1 of this book. It is true that equations (8.8) and (8.9) imply that the interest rate adjusts in order to allocate a given output between consumption and investment. But equation (8.7), which is an equation for the determination of money income, in no way ensures full employment or full capacity utilization. But it was of the essence of the classical position, as interpreted by Keynes, that it assumed continuous full employment. Hence we must conclude that Hicks has misrepresented classical economics, and therefore we need not accept his conclusions about the ways in which Keynes differed from the classical economists. This is a conclusion with which Keynes agreed:

you are perhaps scarcely fair to the classical view . . . . The inconsistency creeps in, I suggest, as soon as it comes to be generally agreed that the increase in the quantity of money is capable of increasing employment. A strictly brought up classical economist would not, I should say, admit that. (Hicks, 1973, p. 9)

The Clower and Leijonhufvud approach to Keynes has been discussed intermittently through the book. It has been argued that Clower (in Clower, 1965) has made basically two contributions to our understanding of Keynes. First, he has provided a theoretical rationale for the Keynesian consumption function; by this is meant not that Keynes explicitly followed Clower's analysis but that his arguments make it plausible that one should come to adopt a Keynesian consumption function in looking at the specific type of disequilibrium problem Keynes was concerned with. He has also shown that Walras' Law, properly interpreted, need pose no threat to Keynesian economics. Perhaps the major achievement of the paper is to provide a foundation for the rigorous study of economies in disequilibrium; this has led to the disequilibrium macro-economic model building of authors such as Barro and Grossman. However, criticisms of Clower can be made from the exegetical point of view. A distinction ought to be made between Walras' Law, which is what Clower discusses, and Say's Law, which Keynes attacks in his chapter 2. Also, the question why disequilibrium should occur in the first place is not tackled; the implications of a non-clearing labour market are successfully examined, but nowhere is the existence and extent of dis-equilibrium explained.

Leijonhufvud's views have been discussed sporadically throughout the book. The comments have usually been critical and it is concluded that the book adds little to our understanding of Keynes. Nevertheless, the book is stimulating and there is much in it which would not be disputed here. For example, the contention that Keynes placed much greater stress on the efficacy of relative price changes than is often believed to be the case would be accepted here. But as an interpretation of Keynes, there is little or nothing to add to the points already made by Clower. Most of the specific exegetical claims made by Leijonhufvud have been discussed as they have arisen.

It has been noted that the disequilibrium models produced by Barro and Grossman might be regarded as at least partially inspired by Clower's analysis. The question how these models relate to Keynesian economics then naturally arises.

In one sense, the models are very similar to the model expounded by Keynes in the General Theory; however, it could also be argued that there is much in the General Theory which is not captured in these models. Consider, for example, the model presented in the *American Economic Review* in 1971. The model combines Clower's idea, that workers who are constrained in their labour supply will contract their consumption demand, and Patinkin's idea, that firms which are constrained in their supply of output will curtail their demand for labour. Combining the two, a model which enables the level of output and employment in conditions of general excess supply to be determined can be constructed. This model will give us typically Keynesian conclusions; an increase in government spending will increase output and employment. The demand for output will increase and since firms feel constrained in their supply of output, they will willingly supply more output and consequentially demand more labour. Again, as labour is in excess supply, extra labour will be supplied, and this, in turn, will lead to extra consumption demand and the process will continue; there is an increase of output and employment which is a multiple of the initial increase in government spending. If we allow the commodity price level to vary so as to clear the commodity market, we have a model which seems to be very similar to that produced by Keynes, where just the labour market may fail to clear. This is a point recognized by Barro and Grossman (see Barro and Grossman, 1976, p. 89). So in this sense the Barro and Grossman type analysis and Keynesian economics are very similar. However, there is much in the General Theory contained in the models produced by Barro and Grossman (this is not intended as in any way a criticism of Barro and Grossman). Keynes's reasons for constructing a model in which the labour market may not clear include stability considerations in the labour market and arguments against Say's Law, whereas more recent disequilibrium model building has tended to rely on a wage/price rigidity type argument — see, for example, Malinvaud (1977) pp. 9-10. Keynes discusses topics such as the role of uncertainty in justifying an interest-sensitive demand for money function and the factors affecting consumption behaviour; such discussion may appear commonplace today; however at the time of writing, it could be described as both innovative and insightful. Moreover, there is much discussion which goes beyond the discussion of the basic model which it has been argued the General Theory conveys.

The view which has come to be known by the phrase 'neo-classical synthesis' is a commonly held interpretation of Keynes. According to this, Keynes claimed to have demonstrated the possibility of an underemployment equilibrium, where even perfect wage and price flexibility will not be sufficient to restore full employment; this will be the case either if there is a liquidity trap or if expenditure is interest-insensitive. However, this claim is invalid if the implications of the Pigou effect are recognized; this will be sufficient to restore full employment equilibrium even if either of the last mentioned conditions obtain. Hence Keynes's theoretical claim is invalid. However, since the special assumption under which Keynes's analysis is valid (wage rigidity) is the one which actually happens to obtain, Keynes's analysis is still applicable for practical purposes even though theoretically the model is based on highly restrictive assumptions. This book will have achieved one of its aims if it succeeds in showing that such arguments are invalid. Keynes did *not* claim to have established the possibility of an under-employment equilibrium, even if all wages and prices are flexible. What he did do was construct an analytic framework for analyzing the workings of an economy in which one market, the labour market, does not necessarily clear. He was perfectly willing to concede that in certain circumstances, wage and price reductions could lead to an increase in output and employment; the argument based on the Pigou effect is one which uses Keynes's analytical framework. Keynes stresses that his difference from the classical theory is primarily 'a difference of analysis', not necessarily one of conclusions drawn. According to this framework, employment could only increase if either the propensity to consume, the interest rate or the marginal efficiency of capital schedule change. The Pigou effect argument proceeds by arguing that falling wages and prices will tend to restore full employment equilibrium through their effect on the propensity to consume; this then is an argument which presupposes the Keynesian framework and hence cannot be used to undermine it.

Bliss is a writer who has recently written insightfully on Keynesian economics and on some of its recent interpreters. He argues against the view that speculation in security markets, as suggested by Leijonhufvud, might be responsible for the problem of involuntary unemployment, but then goes on to conclude 'we will be able to accept that speculation in security markets, allied to money-wage stickiness, may interfere with a full-employment temporary equilibrium that might otherwise be attained' (see Bliss, 1975, p. 213). There are several things which might be said about such a statement, and the interpretation which such a statement seems to exemplify. First, as argued, *passim*, Keynes did not assume money-wage stickiness. Secondly, Keynes's concentration on the speculative demand for money arises out of the necessity for constructing a justification for an interest sensitive demand for money function; a necessity which arose, as argued in chapter 5, from the particular type of disequilibrium system which Keynes was constructing. One may say that the demand for money function, within the Keynesian framework, is very relevant in enabling the level of employment to be determined, but is not at all relevant when the classical system and the reasons why it is inapplicable to the economies of the type Keynes was concerned with, are being considered.

Bliss's critique of Leijonhufvud is convincing, but we need not agree with Blaug, who when commenting upon Bliss's chapter, writes: 'The upshot is to take us back to a Clowerian interpretation of Keynes' (Blaug, 1975, p. 215). As already argued, Clower provides a rationale for only one part of Keynesian economics, the consumption function. There is much more in Keynesian economics which Clower's dual decision hypothesis does not enable us to understand.

This concludes the discussion of how the interpretation presented here differs from other interpretations. Although by no means all possible interpretations have been discussed, most of the important ones of which the author is aware have been, and it is argued that the present interpretation does differ in important and substantial ways from interpretations presented previously. Novel features which the author would like to stress are as follows: first the idea that Keynes's argument based on money illusion is an attack on the way in which the effects of collective bargaining were incorporated into the classical theory of the labour market. Secondly, that his main argument against the classical theory of the labour market involves stability considerations. Thirdly, the interpretation of Say's Law and the way it fits into the classical system. Fourthly, the argument that many of the salient features of the General Theory can in some way be attributed to or derived from the specific disequilibrium structure of his theory. Fifthly, the argument that uncertainty is relevant in Keynes primarily in underpinning the liquidity preference theory of the rate of interest. Sixthly, the argument that the liquidity trap and an unstable marginal efficiency of capital schedule are mentioned in the General Theory, but that they are not considered to be in any sense a source of Keynes's divergence from the classics.

PART III

The next question to be considered is that of the relevance of Keynesian economics for today. Arguments have frequently been presented for the redundancy or irrelevancy of Keynesian economics — see, for example, Eltis's spirited attack (Eltis, 1976). However, the reasons given have often been unconvincing. The position to be taken here is that the Keynesian framework is relevant in the sense that it provides a paradigm and a way of thinking about economic problems which still underlies much macro-economic reasoning and discussion of policy issues; most of the criticisms of Keynesian economics heard today relate not to the basic framework itself, but can be incorporated within that framework appropriately modified and extended. In the following section, a number of criticisms of Keynesian economics will be presented and it will be argued that they should all lead to modifications of the basic Keynesian framework, rather than to its abandonment. A number of misconceptions about what Keynes's framework does or does not entail will be discussed; for example, it will be argued that acceptance of the Keynesian framework in no way entails acceptance of the view that it is possible to 'fine-tune' the economy or that there is or is not a trade-off between inflation and unemployment.

The first criticism of Keynesian economics is either that it is invalid in times of inflation or that it cannot explain inflation. However, the Keynesian framework did generate the concept of the inflationary gap, which proved particularly useful in explaining the inflation of World War II. Keynes discusses such matters in his *How to Pay for the War* (Keynes, 1940). It was only with post-war inflation that Keynesian economics seemed unable to cope. But this is perhaps not too surprising; as we have argued, in Keynesian economics the money-wage is exogenous; its level (and rate of change) are left unexplained; Keynesian economics does not pretend to be able to predict the rate of inflation. It is compatible with many theories of inflation and these can be combined with the main body of Keynesian theory in order to explain the level and rate of change of the money-wage. For example, a Phillips curve could relate the rate of money-wage change to the level of unemployment; hence, given an initial money-wage, the time path of the money-wage can be derived from a Keynesian type model. So the criticism that Keynesian economics cannot explain inflation is not damaging; it was not designed to explain inflation and does not attempt to do so; it can be combined with any theory of inflation which is thought appropriate. However, it may also be thought that inflation has undesirable consequences for some of the assumptions made by Keynes in writing his book. The principal implication that inflation has in this context is that it forces us to distinguish between the real and the nominal interest rate. It has sometimes been held that Keynes's theory is in error for failing to make this distinction and to follow through its implications. (Keynes does seem to recognize the distinction, but seems to reject the implications which are normally thought to follow from it — this has already been discussed in our chapter 5.) For example, it might be argued that it is the real rate of interest which is relevant for investment, whereas it is the nominal rate of interest which is determined in the money market, so that Keynes's theory is justified only on the implausible assumption of a zero rate of inflation. However, there is no need for us to accept this implication; Keynes's theoretical framework can be modified to include the distinction between the real and the nominal interest rate. The first step in such a modification might be to postulate exogenous inflationary expectations; these might enter as an argument into the demand for money function, and given these inflationary expectations, the interest rate would be determined in the money market. With the nominal interest rate determined, the expected real interest rate and hence the level of investment are also determined. The second step might be to introduce a theory of inflation, perhaps in the way discussed above. With the rate of inflation endogenized, inflationary expectations can also be endogenized, via some sort of adaptive expectations mechanism. This would incorporate the effects of inflation in a reasonably satisfactory form. The resultant model would still be a Keynesian model, as the term is used here; the labour market could still fail to clear and the level of aggregate demand would be the major explanatory variable of the level of output and employment. The recognition of inflation and its implications need in no way cause abandonment of the basic Keynesian paradigm.

Another criticism of the basic Keynesian model is that it fails to take into account changes in the levels of some of the stock components of the model, even though these changes may be endogenous. For example, the point is often made that the Keynesian model assumes a fixed capital stock whereas there may well be a positive volume of net investment taking place in the economy, which, by definition, changes the capital stock. But the same point can and should be made with respect to the other stock variables which appear in the model. The money supply and the stock of bonds are also likely to change over time. If there is a budget surplus or deficit, then the level of government indebtedness must change; this will involve a change either in the money stock or in the bond stock or in both. Furthermore, one would expect the changes in these stocks to have economic effects. The change in money or bonds is likely to affect wealth and hence consumer behaviour. The demand for money is likely to be affected as well. But again, these considerations do not call for a rejection of the Keynesian paradigm; the basic short-run equilibrium conditions remain unaltered; what now needs to be considered is the long-run dynamic behaviour of the economy, when the various rules whereby the asset stocks change and the ways in which they affect the economy are specified. This area is now the subject of a burgeoning literature; relevant contributors include Turnovsky (1977) and Currie (1976).

Keynesian economics has also been accused of concentrating excessively on a closed economy and of ignoring the complications caused by the existence of an open economy. Again, the approach taken here is that recognition of the facts of an open economy in no way causes us to abandon the Keynesian framework but it does lead us, however, to expand and extend it. Much has been done in this area as well. A large amount of the post-war work on the balance of payments has consisted of the incorporation of Keynesian factors into the theory of the balance of payments. For example, both the foreign trade multiplier and the absorption approach to the balance of payments may be regarded as applications of the Keynesian type framework to the problems of an open economy. Indeed, the framework might be regarded as particularly appropriate for analyzing the problems of an open economy.

It has sometimes been suggested that Keynes's analysis provides the basis for the view that it is possible for the authorities to 'fine-tune' the economy. His analysis certainly does justify the view that in many situations government action may be *necessary* if a long-drawn-out recession is to be avoided. It does not follow that a government demand management policy can be devised which is *sufficient* to ensure that the economy can stay close to full employment. Indeed, since Keynes emphasized the precariousness of investment, it is probable that he would have rejected the view that the government can 'fine-tune' the economy; perhaps it is for this reason that he advocated a 'somewhat comprehensive social-isation of investment' as 'the only means of securing an approximation to full employment' (G.T., p. 378).

Our earlier discussion will enable us to dismiss the suggestion that we should attribute the view that there may be a trade-off between unemployment and inflation to Keynes or to Keynesian economics. For we have seen that Keynes had no specific theory of inflation in mind when writing the General Theory; he assumed an exogenous money-wage and his theory is compatible with a large number of theories of inflation. It is perhaps plausible that both the concept of fine-tuning and the suggestion of a trade-off between inflation and unemployment should have arisen in the discussion of unemployment and the appropriate policies to pursue in the light of it, and hence it is no surprise that these views have come to be associated with Keynesian economics; however, they are by no means entailed by the theory presented by Keynes.

Perhaps we should comment here on the implications of 'rational expectations'. In recent years much has been done on constructing macro-economic models in which agents form their expectations rationally. (By this it is meant that economic agents use some sort of economic theory for formulating their expectations about the future values of a variable — normally the theory is the actual theory of how the variable is determined in the model itself.) It has sometimes been argued that this has radical consequences for macro-economics and in particular shows that active stabilization or counter-cyclical policy by the government is impossible. One should perhaps be extremely wary of drawing such a conclusion. It can be argued that many of the conclusions of the rational expectations theorists are due not to the assumption of rational expectations but to the accompanying assumptions of market clearing and price flexibility. If these assumptions are not made, then Keynesian-type problems may continue to occur in such an economy. This, in particular, has been argued in a paper by Neary and Stiglitz (1979), who introduce rational expections into a two-period Barro and Grossman type model with rationing. They show that under certain circumstances rational expectations may in fact enhance rather than diminish the effectiveness of government stabilization policies.

So, the position taken here is that Keynes's analytical framework is by no means inadequate for application to present-day economic problems, and that it has perhaps suffered unjustly because of its association with certain by now somewhat discredited economic doctrines. It may well be that the precise simplifications made by Keynes in the General Theory are not appropriate to economic conditions today; however, this does not mean that his framework should be abandoned, but rather that it should be extended and modified; much extension and modification has in fact been done in the post-Keynesian era. Many of the concepts and ideas introduced by Keynes remain at the centre of contemporary macro-economic thinking; notions such as the concepts of aggregate demand and of the consumption function still underlie the way macro-economic problems are discussed and debated today. So, in this sense, Keynesian economics is still relevant for today.

The interpretation presented in this book is, it is claimed, novel and incorporates all the diverse elements which are normally regarded as salient features of Keynesian economics. It is not for the author to judge this claim. However, in the last section of the chapter, it is perhaps worthwhile to discuss some of the implications this interpretation might have and to focus on possible areas for further development. In particular, two areas will be discussed: the role of money in the economy and the theory of the movement of the money-wage.

As argued in this book, primarily in chapter 5, the reasons why Keynes thought money to be important are complex and perhaps can best, but inadequately, be summarized by the statement that for Keynes, money is important because of the fact that it is a non-reproducible store of value *and* because of its liquidity properties. Research on the role of money has concentrated, perhaps excessively, on the medium of exchange function of money. The analysis presented here suggests that other properties of money deserve attention as well. Moreover, Keynes's discussion of the 'essential properties of interest and money' is by no means clear and it is by no means obvious that his conclusions are in fact justified. Hence it seems that more work on both the analytic and the exegetical aspects of the problem are required. Developments in this area might provide a link between the medium of exchange function of money and the other properties of money which are regarded as important.

The other potential area for development concerns the behaviour of the money-wage. As has been stressed repeatedly in this book, the labour market is the only market in Keynesian economics which may persistently fail to clear. This may create problems for the theory of the movement of and the determination of the money-wage; problems which perhaps have not been recognized until recently. But considerations such as the following may be relevant: the assumption that trading takes place at one price in disequilibrium is incompatible with the assumption that individual traders are optimizing agents. For one would expect that agents who are constrained from transacting the amounts they would like to transact at market prices would be prepared to pay a higher price (accept a lower price) in order to move towards their desired transactions bundle. There certainly will be traders on the opposite side of the market who would prefer to transact at these prices. Hence the law of one price, or Jevons's 'law of indifference', which states that a homogenous good will sell at a uniform price will no longer hold in disequilibrium. However, special conditions must prevail if two different prices are to persist in a market for a homogenous good; for one would expect that those who are initially selling at the lower price to attempt to sell at the higher price and vice versa for those who were initially buying at the higher price. If this is not to result in the collapse of the price structure, something must prevent this process from being successful. It could be that informational deficiencies prevent this process from being carried out, or that transactions costs perform a similar function, or that there is some form of non-price rationing scheme. Obviously, these features require further investigation, but it is to be hypothesized that factors such as informational deficiencies and transactions costs will be particularly important in explaining some of the features of the labour market which tend to puzzle economists. In recent years, much attention has been given to the role of information and of informational deficiencies in economic analysis; the hypothesis presented here is that these deficiencies may be particularly relevant for markets in disequilibrium and for the institutional structures which may develop in persistent disequilibrium.

Bibliography

A. A. Alchian (1955), 'The rate of interest: Fisher's rate of return over cost and Keynes's internal rate of return', *American Economic Review*.

A. A. Alchian (1969), 'Information costs, pricing and resource unemployment', *Western Economic Journal*.

K. J. Arrow and F. H. Hahn (1971), *General Competitive Analysis*, Holden Day.

R. J. Barro and H. I. Grossman (1974), 'Suppressed inflation and the supply multiplier', *Review of Economic Studies*.

R. J. Barro and H. I. Grossman (1976), *Money, Employment and Inflation*, Cambridge University Press.

R. J. Barro (1974), 'Are government bonds net wealth?', *Journal of Political Economy*.

W. J. Baumol (1952), 'The transactions demand for cash: an inventory-theoretic approach', *Quarterly Journal of Economics*.

J. P. Benassy (1975), 'Disequilibrium exchange in barter and monetary economies', *Economic Inquiry*.

M. Blaug (1968), *Economic Theory in Retrospect*, Heinemann.

M. Blaug (1975), 'Discussion', in J. M. Parkin and A. R. Nobay (eds), *Current Economic Problems*, Cambridge University Press.

A. S. Blinder and R. W. Solow (1973), 'Does fiscal policy matter?', *Journal of Public Economics*.

C. J. Bliss (1975), 'The reappraisal of Keynes' economics: an appraisal', in J. M. Parkin and A. R. Nobay (eds), *Current Economic Problems*, Cambridge University Press.

R. Brenner (1979), 'Unemployment, justice, and Keynes's "general theory"', *Journal of Political Economy*.

J. F. Brothwell (1975), 'A simple Keynesian's response to Leijonhufvud', *Bulletin of Economic Research*.

S. K. Chakrabati (1979), *The Two-Sector General Theory Model*, Macmillan.

V. Chick (1978), 'The nature of the Keynesian revolution: a reassessment', *Australian Economic Papers*.

R. W. Clower (1969), *Monetary Theory*, Penguin.

R. W. Clower (1965), 'The Keynesian counter-revolution: a theoretical appraisal' in F. H. Hahn and F. Brechling (eds), *The Theory of Interest Rates*, Macmillan, pp. 103-25 and in Clower (1969).

R. W. Clower (1967), 'A reconsideration of the micro-foundations of monetary theory', *Western Economic Journal*, reprinted in Clower (1969).

A. Coddington (1976), 'Keynesian economics: the search for first principles', *Journal of Economic Literature*.

D. Currie (1976), 'Macroeconomic policy and government financing: a survey of recent developments' in M. J. Artis and A. R. Nobay (eds), *Studies in Contemporary Economic Analysis: Vol. I*, Croom Helm.

P. Davidson (1978), *Money and the Real World*, Macmillan.

W. Eltis (1976), 'The failure of the Keynesian conventional wisdom', *Lloyds Bank Review*.

J. S. Flemming (1973), 'The consumption function when capital markets are imperfect: the permanent income hypothesis reconsidered', *Oxford Economic Papers*.

J. S. Flemming (1974), 'Wealth effects in Keynesian models', *Oxford Economic Papers*.

M. Friedman (1974), 'A theoretical framework for monetary analysis' in R. J. Gordon (ed.), *Milton Friedman's Monetary Framework*, Chicago.

R. T. Froyen (1976), 'The aggregative structure of Keynes's General Theory', *Quarterly Journal of Economics*.

H. I. Grossman (1972), 'Was Keynes a "Keynesian"? A review article', *Journal of Economic Literature*.

H. I. Grossman (1974), 'Effective demand failures: a comment', *Swedish Journal of Economics*.

F. H. Hahn (1977), 'Keynesian economics and general equilibrium theory: reflections on some current debates' in G. C. Harcourt (ed.), *The Microeconomic Foundations of Macroeconomics*, Macmillan.

A. H. Hansen (1953), *A Guide to Keynes*, McGraw Hill.

J. R. Hicks (1937), 'Mr. Keynes and the "Classics"', *Econometrica*.

J. R. Hicks (1967), *Critical Essays in Monetary Theory*, Oxford University Press.

J. R. Hicks (1973), 'Recollections and documents', *Economica*.

J. R. Hicks (1974), *The Crisis in Keynesian Economics*, Basil Blackwell.

R. Jackman (1974), 'Keynes and Leijonhufvud', *Oxford Economic Papers*.

H. G. Johnson (1964), 'Monetary theory and Keynesian economics' reprinted in Clower (1969).

H. G. Johnson (1969), 'Inside money, outside money, income, wealth and welfare in monetary theory', *Journal of Money, Credit and Banking*.

R. F. Kahn (1931), 'The relation of home investment and unemployment', *Economic Journal*.

J. M. Keynes (1923), *A Tract on Monetary Reform*, Macmillan.

J. M. Keynes (1930), *A Treatise on Money* (2 vols), Macmillan.

J. M. Keynes (1937a), 'The general theory of employment', *Quarterly Journal of Economics* reprinted in Clower (1969).

J. M. Keynes (1937b), 'Alternative theories of the rate of interest', *Economic Journal.*

J. M. Keynes (1940), *How to Pay for the War*, Macmillan.

L. R. Klein (1966), *The Keynesian Revolution*, Macmillan.

R. H. Kuenne (1963), *The Theory of General Economic Equilibrium*, Princeton.

A. Leijonhufvud (1967), 'Keynes and the Keynesians: a suggested interpretation', *American Economic Review*, reprinted in Clower (1969).

A. Leijonhufvud (1968), *On Keynesian Economics and the Economics of Keynes*, Oxford University Press.

W. W. Leontief (1936), 'The fundamental postulate of Mr. Keynes' monetary theory of unemployment', *Quarterly Journal of Economics.*

A. Lerner (1952), 'The essential properties of interest and money', *Quarterly Journal of Economics.*

S. A. Lippman and J. J. McCall (1976), 'The economics of job search: a survey, *Economic Inquiry.*

B. J. Loasby (1976), *Choice, Complexity and Ignorance*, Cambridge University Press.

E. Malinvaud (1977), *The Theory of Unemployment Reconsidered*, Basil Blackwell.

J. E. Meade (1978), *The Structure and Reform of Direct Taxation*, Allen and Unwin.

H. P. Minsky (1975), *John Maynard Keynes*, Columbia University Press.

F. Modigliani (1944), 'Liquidity preference and the theory of interest and money', *Econometrica.*

D. Moggridge (ed.) (1973), *The General Theory and After. Part II: Defence and Development*, Vol. XIV of *Keynes's Collected Writings.*

J. P. Neary and J. E. Stiglitz (1979), 'Towards a reconstruction of Keynesian economics: expectations and constrained equilibria', unpublished paper.

D. Patinkin (1965), *Money, Interest and Prices*, Harper and Row.

D. Patinkin (1969), 'Money and wealth: a review article', *Journal of Economic Literature*.

D. Patinkin (1976), 'Keynes' monetary thought: a study of its development', *History of Political Economy*.

D. Patinkin (1977), 'The process of writing the General Theory: a critical survey' in D. Patinkin and J. C. Leith (eds), *Keynes, Cambridge and the General Theory*, Macmillan.

D. Patinkin (1978b), 'Keynes and the multiplier', *Manchester School*.

D. Patinkin (1978b), *Keynes and the Multiplier*, Manchester School of Business Studies.

D. Patinkin (1979), 'Keynes' theory of effective demand', *Economic Inquiry*.

E. S. Phelps (ed.) (1976), *Microeconomic Foundations of Employment and Inflation Theory*, W. W. Norton, New York.

J. H. Power (1959), 'Price expectations, money illusion, and the real balance effect', *Journal of Political Economy*.

D. L. Roberts (1978), 'Patinkin, Keynes and aggregate supply and demand analysis', *History of Political Economy*.

M. Rothschild (1973), 'Models of market organisation with imperfect information: a survey', *Journal of Political Economy*.

H. Scarf (1960), 'Some examples of global instability of the competitive equilibrium', *International Economic Review*.

G. L. S. Shackle (1973), 'Keynes and today's establishment in economic theory: a view', *Journal of Economic Literature*.

T. Sowell (1972), *Say's Law*, Princeton University Press.

T. Sowell (1974), *Classical Economics Reconsidered*, Princeton University Press.

E. Shapiro (1978), *Macroeconomic Activity*, Harcourt Brace.

J. Trevithick (1976), 'Money wage inflexibility and the Keynesian labour supply function', *Economic Journal*.

S. J. Turnovsky (1977), *Macroeconomic analysis and stabilization policy*, Cambridge University Press

J. Tobin (1958), 'Liquidity preference as behaviour towards risk', *Review of Economic Studies*.

E. R. Weintraub (1979), *Microfoundations*, Cambridge University Press.

L. B. Yeager (1973) 'The Keynesian diversion', *Western Economic Journal*.

Index